Words of Life

THE BIBLE DAY BY DAY WITH THE SALVATION ARMY

ADVENT EDITION SEPTEMBER-DECEMBER 2001

Hodder & Stoughton
LONDON SYDNEY AUCKLAND
AND THE SALVATION ARMY

First published in Great Britain in 2001

10 9 8 7 6 5 4 3 2 1

British Library Cataloguing in Publication Data
A record for this book is available from the British Library

ISBN 0 340 75701 9

Printed and bound in Great Britain by
Omnia

Hodder & Stoughton
A Division of Hodder Headline Ltd
338 Euston Road
London NW1 3BH

POHUTUKAWA CHRISTMAS

In this southern place
pohutukawa stands all year
green and murmuring
wind-whipped
clinging to rocky shorelines.
But when pohutukawa breaks
glorious red
against a clear blue sky
to the roar of rolling surf
we know Christmas has come!
Time to light the barbecue
slap on sunscreen
and celebrate.

Pohutukawa Christ,
You stand in our midst all year
singing your ever-green song of love.
But at Christmas you break out
blood-red, flesh-soft
to the sound of a baby breathing.

Gift beyond description
we kneel to welcome you.

Barbara Sampson
New Zealand

CONTENTS

MAJOR BARBARA SAMPSON WRITES . . .

For any child, the countdown to Christmas happens far too slowly. When I was young, those days seemed much too long and the nights even longer. But something has happened over the years. I've slowed down and the days seem to have sped up. Now, Christmas comes far too quickly and I long to hold it back so that I can savour its coming.

Advent means 'coming' and is the name given to the four weeks leading up to Christmas. It is the season of wonder, the season of watching and waiting for Jesus' coming. It's difficult to watch and wait and wonder when there is so much to do. Busy schedules and endless lists scream their demands at us, driving us on and giving us little opportunity to rest and be still. But if we don't stop and listen and watch, then we are in danger of missing his coming altogether. We'll put up the decorations, sing the carols, open the gifts, but Advent won't really reach our hearts.

In all the whirl and busyness of these days, I invite you to pause and reflect. Try to listen this year to the story of Jesus' coming as if you are a child, hearing it for the very first time.

> The Word became flesh and made his dwelling among us. We have seen his glory, the glory of the One and Only, who came from the Father, full of grace and truth.
>
> *John 1:14*

May the wonder of his coming and the glory and grace with which he came touch you in a fresh way this Advent, making it truly a season to celebrate.

ABBREVIATIONS USED

AV	Authorised (King James) Version
NIV	New International Version
NRSV	New Revised Standard Version
RSV	Revised Standard Version

SASB	*The Song Book of The Salvation Army*, 1986

PHILIPPIANS – A SONG OF JOY

Introduction

When Paul wrote this letter to the believers at Philippi, he was in prison awaiting a trial whose outcome could result in his execution. If you read this letter expecting to hear the bleak and anguished last words of a condemned prisoner, then you are in for a surprise. This is a letter full of joy. As a friend, Paul writes a personal letter, filled with love and gratitude, to a group of friends, to thank them for the gift of money they had sent him by one of their members. Their gift had brought him joy, but even more, they themselves were a gift in which he rejoiced.

In his lifetime, Paul had faced abject poverty and abundant wealth and everything in between. He had been honoured and humiliated, celebrated and shipwrecked, but he had found a key to living. He had learned to be content as he focused all his attention not on outward circumstances, but on knowing and obeying Christ. Everything else paled in comparison with that passion.

It is out of this passion that he writes, not only to thank his dear friends for their gift, but also to commend the way of joy to them. May God's joy touch you also as you study this gem of a letter.

SATURDAY 1 SEPTEMBER

Of Servants and Saints

Philippians 1:1–11

'Paul and Timothy, servants of Christ Jesus, to all the saints in Christ Jesus at Philippi . . . Grace and peace to you' (vv. 1,2, NIV).

In Paul's day, letters were an important means of communication. Government officials, philosophers and politicians all wrote letters to express their views. Paul's letter to the Philippians was a pastoral letter, thanking them for a gift they had sent to him in prison by Epaphroditus, one of their members. Paul follows the standard format of a letter, giving the name of the sender, the name of the recipient and a greeting, but his opening words in this letter are deeper than formality. They also have theological significance.

First, he describes himself and Timothy as 'servants of Christ Jesus'. The word 'servants' refers not to household help, but to slaves. Paul does not make a distinction between himself as the older, more mature believer and Timothy as younger and less experienced, but states that they stand together as slaves of Christ Jesus. Second, he addresses 'all the saints', that is, all who are set apart as the treasured possession of God, to serve and minister to the needs of others. Thus at the beginning of his letter, Paul provides a model of humility that he will soon explain in greater detail. Third, his greeting of grace and peace is more than just a friendly hello. The grace of the Lord Jesus Christ and peace from God are the results of God's redemptive work on their behalf (see *Rom 5:1–2*).

Paul then outlines the two ways in which he prays for the Philippians. First, with a heart full of joy, he thanks God for their partnership with him in the work of the gospel. Even though their church was not wealthy (*2 Cor 8:2–3*), they gave as no other church had done (*Phil 4:15*) and they continued to stand by him even in his imprisonment. This consistent, practical support has gained them a special place in Paul's heart and confirms to him that God is indeed at work in their lives. Second, he prays that they might grow spiritually, with the result that God will receive glory and praise.

Pray today for another believer, using Paul's pattern of thanksgiving and intercession.

SUNDAY 2 SEPTEMBER

Who May Enter Your Presence?

Psalm 15

'LORD, who may dwell in your sanctuary? Who may live on your holy hill?' (v. 1, NIV).

Psalm 15 is a psalm traditionally used on Ascension Day. It speaks of admission into the presence of God, just as Christ was admitted to the full presence of God when he ascended to heaven (see *Acts 1:9*).

Psalm 15 is made up of a question, an answer and a promise. The question is as relevant today as when it was first asked. What are the conditions for entering into God's presence? The answer is given in a series of positive and negative conditions. Both active goodness and an absence of evil are necessary.

The first three conditions listed are positive – such a person must walk blamelessly, do right and speak the truth. The next three conditions repeat the first three but in negative terms – anyone wanting to enter God's presence must speak no slander, do no wrong to his neighbour and spread no gossip. The next essential characteristic is that he despises the habitual evildoer, but honours the person who fears God. This God-seeker has indicated not merely a determination to do good, but has sworn a solemn oath not to do wrong.

The last two characteristics are very specific. The person who wants to enter God's presence must avoid both usury and bribery. The lending of money at interest normally involved exploitation and abuse. Thus Hebrew law prevented loans on interest to fellow Hebrews, but permitted them in business transactions with foreigners.

The psalm concludes with the promise, 'He who does these things will never be shaken.' Human enemies and the ups and downs of life were constantly shaking the psalmists. They often lamented the apparent victory of the godless over the godly. But beyond these temporary 'shakings', they knew that there is for the godly 'a place of quiet rest, near to the heart of God'.

To reflect on

Even in this day, our use of words and money says a great deal about our character and our faith.

MONDAY 3 SEPTEMBER

No Ordinary Prisoner

Philippians 1:12–30

'For to me, to live is Christ and to die is gain' (v. 21, NIV).

The Philippians had heard that Paul was in prison and were distressed by the news. How was he? Were his physical needs being met? The visit of Epaphroditus with the gift from the church was probably prompted by their concern. Paul knows their heart and writes to assure them that, in fact, his imprisonment has advanced rather than hindered the progress of the gospel. The news has swept through the palace guard and others who live close by that he is no ordinary prisoner. He has had opportunity to explain that his imprisonment is for the cause of Christ.

What's more, the gospel has been advanced by his imprisonment because most of his Christian brothers have taken courage from his example, and are now proclaiming the word with greater boldness. He admits there are two groups among these Christian brothers. One group, knowing the truth about Paul's imprisonment, is motivated by love. The other group, motivated by competition and selfish ambition, is hoping that their preaching will worsen his suffering. But Paul's remarkable conclusion is that 'whether from false motives or true, Christ is preached' and in that he rejoices. For this man, whose joy was linked to the advancement of the gospel more than his own physical situation, this is a win-win situation!

Paul not only rejoices at how God is using his present circumstances to advance the gospel, but also declares that he will continue to rejoice. On one level, the final outcome of his imprisonment is uncertain, but on another level his future circumstances are quite certain, for he knows that Christ will be exalted, 'whether by life or by death'. If he is delivered from prison as a result of their prayers, then that means continued opportunity for the gospel. If he is not released but is executed, that will still be a deliverance, into the very presence of Christ. Again it is win-win all the way.

To reflect on

Paul may be in chains but the gospel goes forward freely. 'Whether this or that', the gospel is advanced. Is yours a similar win-win situation?

TUESDAY 4 SEPTEMBER

'He Made Himself Nothing'

Philippians 2:1–11

'Your attitude should be the same as that of Christ Jesus' (v. 5, NIV).

In commending a spirit of unity, compassion and humility among his readers, Paul cites the greatest example he could give – the Lord Jesus Christ himself. In a great credal hymn, full of colour and movement, he describes how Jesus 'made himself nothing'. Jesus, present with the Father in creation, was heir to all the riches of heaven. But he came to earth as the incarnate Jesus, God clothed in flesh. Instead of grasping, he gave and gave until he was empty. From the place of honour and glory with the Father, Jesus modelled to those he called to follow him a leadership style that was humble, servant-like, characterised by a towel and basin. His humility took him all the way to death, a horrifying death usually reserved for the worst criminals.

This downward movement from honour to humiliation is followed by a great upward sweep as Paul describes the glorified Christ. The obedience of Christ the Son was honoured by the Father as he raised him from the dead and exalted him to the highest place where he will receive glory and worship from every creature in heaven and on earth and under the earth. 'Hallelujah', our hearts cry.

But hold on a moment! Paul is not just waxing eloquent. He is writing to people who share a common life in Christ. 'If you have any encouragement . . . any comfort . . . any fellowship . . . any tenderness and compassion', then 'your attitude should be the same as that of Christ Jesus'. What would such an example of 'making himself nothing' look like for the Philippians? He tells them bluntly: it would look like unity and humility with each believer lovingly looking out for the interests of others.

What would it look like for believers and for you and me today? In a world where personal rights are held to be sacred, a call to emptiness and nothingness sounds extremely uncomfortable.

To reflect on

Do you want to be great? Then follow the example of Jesus, let go, take the lowest place, pour yourself out and become nothing.

WEDNESDAY 5 SEPTEMBER

Work Out Your Salvation

Philippians 2:12–18

'Continue to work out your salvation with fear and trembling' (v. 12, NIV).

Applying Christ's incomparable example to the Philippians' situation, Paul encourages them to continue their good record of obedience, whether he is with them or not, and to work out their salvation 'with fear and trembling'. The word 'work' immediately puts us on alert. Is this the same person who wrote to the Ephesian Christians, 'It is by grace you have been saved, through faith – and this is not from yourselves, it is the gift of God – not by works, so that no-one can boast' (*Eph 2:8–9*)? Is he now contradicting himself?

To use the illustration of a clock, imagine that the Philippians' pre-Christian days were in the half-hour coming up to midday. The initiative of bringing them to that point in time was in every way the work of God. He drew them, wooed them and spoke to them through people like Paul and Timothy. The moment of their salvation was the midday point. This momentous thing happened, not because of what they had done or earned, nor because of any deal they had signed with God, but simply because of his unmerited grace and favour poured out upon them.

Now, Paul is saying, as you live in the light of that salvation experience, in the time period after midday as it were, take your faith seriously, live out the implications of what it means to be Christian, and make every effort to guard against divisions and discord in the Church. In all your relationships watch your tongue and guard against a murmuring, argumentative spirit. This may well feel like work, but the effort on your part is evidence of God's work within you. And it needs to be done 'with fear and trembling' because such seriousness will demonstrate that you are genuine believers, committed to the gospel. When lived like this, your lives will be like stars shining against a dark background of unbelief.

So Paul writes to the Philippians, his words sounding remarkably relevant for believers today!

To reflect on

My life is God's gift to me. What I do with it is my gift to God.

THURSDAY 6 SEPTEMBER

A Load of Rubbish

Philippians 3:1–11

'I consider everything a loss compared to the surpassing greatness of knowing Christ Jesus my Lord, for whose sake I have lost all things' (v. 8, NIV).

The regal procession moved slowly along the spacious aisle of the great auditorium. From the awe-struck audience came gasps of wonder at the jewel-studded crowns, the rich ermine shawls, the glorious purple robes made from softest velvet. As the noble figures made their way onto the platform, the admiring hush of the audience turned into thunderous applause, but then suddenly stopped in shock as the people in the procession pulled off their crowns, their robes and shawls and stuffed them into rubbish bags!

Paul had done something similarly shocking. He had been an impressive figure. His fine upbringing, nationality, family background, inheritance, orthodoxy, privileges, accomplishments and personal standing had made him a giant of a man. He had carried these distinctions like a glittering, star-studded victory wreath.

But in a blinding moment of revelation a great reversal had happened (see *Acts 9:3–16*). On the road leading into Damascus and in the subsequent prayer ministry of Ananias, he had encountered the very Jesus whom he had persecuted. The impeccable credentials that he had carried so proudly had become no more than a load of rubbish. The treasures that once throbbed with life for him now lay at his feet, as worthless as dead leaves. A new passion now claimed his heart and every ounce of energy he possessed – knowing Jesus.

For Paul, life had changed from credentials to Christ, belonging to him, receiving his righteousness, sharing his sufferings, anticipating resurrection and eternal life. A modern songwriter tells Paul's story this way:

All I once held dear, built my life upon,
All this world reveres, and wars to own,
All I once thought gain I have counted loss;
Spent and worthless now, compared to this.

Knowing You, Jesus, knowing You,
There is no greater thing.
You're my all, You're the best,
You're my joy and righteousness,
And I love You, Lord.

Graham Kendrick[1]

FRIDAY 7 SEPTEMBER

A Race with a Goal

Philippians 3:12–4:1

'Therefore, my brothers, you whom I love and long for, my joy and crown, that is how you should stand firm in the Lord, dear friends!' (4:1, NIV).

I was never athletic. Sports days and physical education classes at school were a nightmare to be avoided by official note from my mother, if at all possible! But the imagery of athletes in training that Paul uses to describe the Christian life makes even me interested. This is a race that everyone can win.

Having written so personally about the things he has gladly let go of in order to gain Christ, Paul is anxious not to give the impression that he has arrived at spiritual perfection. 'I'm still on the journey,' he says, 'refusing to rest on past successes and pressing on toward the goal.' He is single-minded and determined, like an athlete who has spent months in training. The prize upon which he is so focused is the call of God to be among those, both Jew and Gentile, who will one day stand before God, forgiven and set free because of their identification with Jesus Christ. The need to attain this goal absorbs every ounce of energy he possesses.

Like a coach urging on his team, he calls the Philippians to pursue Christlikeness by following his example. 'Press on... take hold... strain forward,' he urges. There are others who will distract and discourage. These enemies of Christ are the 'dogs' he referred to earlier (*3:2*) who put all their efforts into following the outward signs of religion, while keeping their hearts untouched.

Paul reminds his readers that they are citizens of a heavenly commonwealth. The goal of their existence will be reached on the day when the Lord Jesus Christ returns. When that happens, he says, Christ will transform their 'lowly bodies', their fallen existence, into his glorious existence, and Paul's beloved friends in Philippi who are already his joy and crown will become his crown in the fullest sense. For Paul, that honour will be far greater than the crown of leaves that is placed on the head of an athlete on the victory dais.

Today, run well, and as you do, look for someone else whom you can coach and encourage.

SATURDAY 8 SEPTEMBER

And Finally...

Philippians 4:2–23

'And the peace of God, which transcends all understanding, will guard your hearts and your minds in Christ Jesus' (v. 7, NIV).

A huge crowd of people from the business world registers to hear the dynamic motivational speaker from the large overseas corporation. Each person unhesitatingly pays the thousand-dollar fee for the two-day workshop. Topics to be covered, with impressive audio-visual presentation techniques, include:

- Conflict resolution
- Walking away from worry
- The secret of a contented life
- Essential qualities of leadership
- The practice of positive thinking
- How to respond graciously to generosity
- How to have a powerful influence on others.

The apostle Paul was never advertised as a motivational speaker, but from a prison in Rome he wrote a letter of thanks to a church in Philippi and just happened to cover the above topics in his letter. This final chapter contains some helpful guidelines for Christian living today.

Having urged his readers to 'conduct yourselves in a manner worthy of the gospel of Christ' (*1:27*), Paul continues to explain what that means. Without taking sides, he names two of his Philippian readers and urges them to put the interests of each other first and 'in the Lord' to drop their quarrel (*4:2*). He then addresses the whole congregation who, he knows, are suffering under opposition from their pagan neighbours. He urges them to maintain an attitude of joy 'in the Lord' at all times and to adopt an approach of gentle non-retaliation toward their persecutors. Keeping in mind that the Lord is near, they should replace their anxiety with thankful prayer. If they follow this advice, he says, then the peace of God will keep guard of their hearts and minds.

Paul closes his letter on a personal note. He thanks them for their financial support, while making it clear that his work is neither dependent on, nor motivated by, that support. He may be in prison, but he is not in need, for he has learned to be content, no matter what. With a word of greeting and grace, he concludes.

To reflect on

Have you found the secret of a contented life?

SUNDAY 9 SEPTEMBER

The Lord is My Portion

Psalm 16

'You have made known to me the path of life; you will fill me with joy in your presence, with eternal pleasures at your right hand' (v. 11, NIV).

Psalm 16 is both a prayer for safekeeping and a song of trust. The word 'Miktam' (from a word that may mean 'to cover') is used at the head of this and five other psalms of David, all of which begin with a prayer for God's protection (see *Pss 56–60*).

It is hard to tell whether the psalmist is in the midst of the crisis, or whether he is looking back and expressing his confidence in God as a result of being delivered from the crisis. Whatever the situation, he has had to make a choice between worshipping false gods (*v. 4*) and dependence upon the Lord (*v. 2*). In granting him his 'portion' and his 'cup', God has overflowed that cup with blessings. As he reflects on his experience of life, the psalmist uses a metaphor of the allocation of land. He has been awarded 'pleasant places' and a 'delightful inheritance'. God's divine counsel, even during the sleepless night hours, has added to this bountiful experience.

His general reflection on the goodness of life then returns to the particular crisis, either threatening or recently experienced. His confidence in the face of mortal threat is based on the fact that God is both in front of him in protection and also at his right hand, holding him steady in the midst of events that shake him. With such confidence in the Lord, he knows that even the grave cannot rob him of life. If this can be said of David, how much more of David's promised Son! So Peter quotes these words in his sermon at Pentecost (see *Acts 2:25–28*), and declares that David was prophesying of Christ and his Resurrection.

David has found the secret of joy. Far deeper than happiness, which comes and goes depending on external happenings, this joy lasts because it flows from God. For the psalmist, and for believers today, the threefold promise of verse 11 is that God delights to give to his children:

- the path of life
- the presence of the Lord
- pleasures that last forever!

THE NAMES OF JESUS

Introduction

Three months before the birth of their baby, the young couple is combing through the list of names in the Baby Book to find a name for their son or daughter. They need to find a name that is just right, a unique name that will both sum up the child and give the child something to grow into.

A child born into royalty may be given multiple names in honour of the royal family line. Or if the parents think their child is very special, they may give multiple names, such as Henry James Winstone Fotherby-Simms, or Annabel Elizabeth Marguerita Minson-Jones!

A few months out from Christmas, it seems appropriate to look at some of the names that were given to Jesus not three months before but, in some cases, hundreds of years before his birth. His names, with all their variations, number over a hundred, for he was both royalty and very special. Each name speaks something of his nature and the reason for his coming. Each name invites our reflection and our response.

Praise the name of Jesus
Praise the name of Jesus
He's my Rock, he's my Fortress, he's my Deliverer
In him will I trust
Praise the name of Jesus

Roy Hicks[2]

MONDAY 10 SEPTEMBER

Jesus

Matthew 1:18–21

'God . . . gave him the name that is above every name, that at the name of Jesus every knee should bow, in heaven and on earth and under the earth' (Phil 2:9,10, NIV).

The name 'Jesus' which was announced to Mary and Joseph before the baby's birth is a simple name. It is the Greek form of Joshua, which means 'the Lord saves'. It was probably a common name in Jesus' day. But as a name given to this baby, it is a sublime name. Paul had such a profound respect for it that he called it 'the name that is above every name'.

The name is used 600 times in the Gospels alone. The frequent use of the name by the disciples shows that it is a name to *speak*. They followed him, walked with him, listened to him and learned from him. As the apostle John said, 'We knew him.' For those who followed, Jesus' name revealed not only who he was, but also what he was and what he had come to do.

His was a name to speak in authority, as the apostles reported when they returned from their mission, describing how even demons were subject to them through his name (*Luke 10:17*). His was also a name to speak in prayer, for he promised, 'My Father will give you whatever you ask in my name' (*John 16:23*).

In the centuries since his birth, people have discovered that the name of Jesus is a name to *sing*. From the oldest songbooks of the Church, which proclaim the name of Jesus as the 'sweetest anthem ever sung', to modern-day songs that focus on his name, Christians have found delight in the singing of Jesus' name.

His is also a name to *shout*. A young Christian woman was woken suddenly during the night by an intruder who had entered her flat. 'I shouted out the name of Jesus,' she said later. 'I don't know what that name meant to him, but he took off as fast as he could!'

Jesus – speak, sing, shout his name today!

Jesus, what a beautiful name.
Son of God, Son of Man,
Lamb that was slain.
Joy and peace, strength and hope,
Grace that blows all fear away.
Jesus, what a beautiful name.

Tanya Riches[3]

TUESDAY 11 SEPTEMBER

Son of God

Matthew 14:22–33

'Then those who were in the boat worshipped him, saying, "Truly you are the Son of God" ' (v. 33, NIV).

The title 'Son of God' is the divine face of Jesus, expressing his unique relationship with God the Father. Although he frequently referred to God as his Father, often using the familiar term 'Abba' that a child would use for 'Daddy', Jesus seldom spoke of himself as the Son of God. Yet when others used it of him, he accepted the name as belonging to himself.

Angels announced the name. Before his birth they declared that the holy one, Jesus, would be born of a virgin as the Son of God (*Luke 1:34,35*).

God the Father affirmed the name. At Jesus' baptism, God's voice from heaven declared that the one whom John was immersing in the water was his Son. Moreover, he was a loved Son, the delight of his Father (*Luke 3:22*).

Jesus' disciples recognised the name. His teaching and his miracles gave them no other explanation than that he was the Son of God. Individuals such as Nathanael (*John 1:49*) and Martha (*John 11:27*) were among others who declared Jesus to be the Son of God. Demons also recognised his supernatural origin. As soon as they caught sight of Jesus, they cried out the testimony of who he was, but Jesus always silenced them.

His death confirmed the name. The chief priests mocked him as he died. 'Let God rescue him now if he wants him, for he said, "I am the Son of God" ' (*Matt 27:43*). In contrast, the centurion who was guarding Jesus as he died exclaimed, 'Surely he was the Son of God!' (*Matt 27:54*).

His resurrection proved the name. If there had been any doubt before as to his origin, Jesus' resurrection from the dead proved for all time that he is the Son of God (see *Rom 1:4*).

Our confession owns the name. The apostle John wrote, 'He who has the Son has life; he who does not have the Son of God does not have life' (*1 John 5:12*).

Let this name of Jesus – Son of God – give you life today!

WEDNESDAY 12 SEPTEMBER

Son of Man

Hebrews 2:14–18

'No-one has ever gone into heaven except the one who came from heaven – the Son of Man' (John 3:13, NIV).

Jesus avoided using the term 'Son of God' in referring to himself, but frequently used the name 'Son of Man'. 'Son of Man' is the human face of Jesus. It not only expressed his personal qualities as a man, but also identified him with the humanity he came to redeem. The title 'Son of Man' concealed his Messiahship, but revealed the purpose of his mission. 'The Son of Man did not come to be served, but to serve, and to give his life as a ransom for many' (*Mark 10:45*). Several verses in Scripture refer to Jesus as a son in a way that connects him firmly to human relationships.

He is called the son of Abraham (*Matt 1:1*). Jesus spoke of Abraham rejoicing at the thought of 'seeing my day' (*John 8:56*). All that was promised to Abraham was ultimately fulfilled in Jesus.

He is called the son of David (*Matt 21:9*). This is a royal title because he would come directly from the line of King David (*2 Sam 7:12–16*).

He is called the son of Joseph (*Luke 3:23*). Luke, the beloved physician, who presumably learned from Mary herself the details of Jesus' conception and birth, is careful to say that Jesus, 'so it was thought', was the son of Joseph. It is a mystery that he was the Son of Man but not the son of a man. Joseph himself received a divine revelation of what his part was to be and, from the time of Jesus' birth, acted with integrity as his human father.

He is called the son of Mary (*Mark 6:3*). He was both her firstborn son and, at the same time, God's son (*Matt 1:25; 2:15*). In the person of Jesus, divinity and humanity combined. Mary's arms were his first home. As he grew 'in wisdom and stature', she guided and nurtured him. Standing by the cross as he died, did she finally understand that her beloved son was also the beloved Son of God?

Jesus, Son of Man, walk with me on my journey today.

THURSDAY 13 SEPTEMBER

Alpha and Omega

Revelation 22:12–17

'I am the Alpha and the Omega, the First and the Last, the Beginning and the End' (v. 13, NIV).

Alpha and Omega, the first and last letters of the Greek alphabet, are used as a grand title of Jesus. As Alpha, Jesus is the beginning point of our relationship with God. 'He [God] chose us in him [Jesus] before the creation of the world to be holy and blameless in his sight' (*Eph 1:4*).

As Alpha, Jesus is the initiator of every new phase of our relationship with God. Author Joyce Huggett wrote, 'God is on the inside of every longing we have after him.' Do you feel the need to pray more, to live with a greater sense of God's presence each day? Jesus is the one who has placed those longings in your heart. Do you want to meet him in every person and every circumstance of this day? He wants that, too, and will open your eyes to see him even in the most unexpected people and places.

As Omega, Jesus is our goal and destination. 'Man's chief end is to glorify God and to enjoy him forever' (*The Shorter Catechism 1647*). What he begins as Alpha, he completes as Omega. The writer to the Hebrews paints a graphic picture of the Christian life as a race in which we are cheered on by those who have run before. 'Let us run with perseverance . . .' he says. 'Let us fix our eyes on Jesus, the author and perfecter of our faith' (*Heb 12:1,2*). In this race, Jesus is both the start and the finish.

If the knitting of winter jerseys was left to me, I know I would have a pile of half-finished garments, begun with determination, then abandoned in discouragement. Jesus, the Alpha and Omega, will never begin something in our lives that he will not finish. We need have no fear of being abandoned like a half-finished jersey! The promise is that 'He who began a good work in you will carry it on to completion' (*Phil 1:6*).

To reflect on

To have Jesus at the beginning and end of the alphabet of our lives is to spell out all the language of heaven.

FRIDAY 14 SEPTEMBER

Word

John 1:1–14

'In the beginning was the Word, and the Word was with God, and the Word was God. He was with God in the beginning' (John 1:1,2, NIV).

Pause for a moment to examine these first two verses of John's Gospel. In two sentences there are twenty-four words, but really a combination of only nine words, all of them just one syllable except for the word 'beginning'. A child could read these two sentences with ease. Their significance, however, has stretched the most brilliant minds and produced countless books and commentaries.

John begins his Gospel, not by introducing himself and giving his credentials for writing, but by introducing Jesus whom he calls the Word. Cleverly, John uses a term that would be meaningful to all his readers. Greeks used the term 'word' not only of the spoken word but also of the unspoken word, the word still in the mind, namely the reason. Jews used the term as a way of referring to God. John therefore used the term 'Word' (in Greek, *logos*) to declare that Jesus in human form is both the collection of thoughts in the mind of God, and the words by which those thoughts are expressed.

John may have been thinking of the beginning of Scripture where God's voice spoke creation into being. Eight times in the Genesis narrative of creation, the words 'And God said' are repeated, like the refrain of a great creation hymn. John gathers up all that God has said into a single saying, and proclaims that this word is Jesus. As the Word, Jesus is God's will and wisdom in the flesh, the very expression of God in human form.

- Do you want to know what God looks like? Then look at Jesus.
- Do you want to know what God sounds like? Then listen to Jesus.
- Do you want to hear what God says? Then listen deeply to Jesus, for he is God spelling himself out in a language that everyone can understand.

Jesus is the word of God:

- ***a passionate word (John 3:16)***
- ***a pertinent word (John 6:68–69)***
- ***a personal word (John 1:12)***
- ***a perfect word (Heb 7:28)***
- ***a permanent word (Heb 7:24–25)***

SATURDAY 15 SEPTEMBER

Root of Jesse

Isaiah 11:1–10

'Isaiah says, "The Root of Jesse will spring up, one who will arise to rule over the nations; the Gentiles will hope in him" ' (Rom 15:12, NIV).

Put a New Testament in the hands of a new Christian and they will probably skim over the long genealogy at the start of Matthew's Gospel. But put that genealogy in the hands of a believer with a knowledge of the Scriptures and they will see here a collection of gems sparkling with blessing.

Jesus is referred to as the Root of Jesse or the Root of David, names which appear in Matthew's genealogy (*Matt 1:5,6*). In the horticultural world, a root is that part of the plant below the surface of the earth that draws up nourishment from the soil. The word 'root' is used in this way in Scripture (see *Matt 13:6*), but the term is also used symbolically of the origin or source of people and ancestors (see *Rom 11:16–18*).

When Isaiah described the coming Messiah as the Root of Jesse, he was referring to Jesse, the father of David. By the time of Jesus, the line of Jesse had fallen into obscurity, like a mighty tree that has fallen. Job said, 'At least there is hope for a tree: If it is cut down, it will sprout again, and its new shoots will not fail' (*Job 14:7*). And sprout it did.

The grandfather of Jesse was Boaz, a Jew; his grandmother was Ruth, a Moabitess. Their son Obed, father of Jesse, had mingled blood of both Jew and Gentile in his veins. Thus Jesus the Messiah, from the root of Jesse, was born to a Jewish mother and recognised as a Jew from the tribe of Judah (*Matt 2:1,2*), but because of his human descent from Obed and Jesse, also had the mingled blood of both Jew and Gentile. That is why Paul could shout with confidence, 'There is neither Jew nor Greek . . . for you are all one in Christ Jesus' (*Gal 3:28*).

Jesus, the Root of Jesse, is a Man for all nations!

To reflect on

Today, as you look at someone of another race, consider that this person is not a stranger, but your brother or sister in Christ.

SUNDAY 16 SEPTEMBER

A Prayer for Deliverance

Psalm 17

'Show the wonder of your great love, you who save by your right hand those who take refuge in you from their foes' (v. 7, NIV).

Desperate cries, racing pulse, heaving chest, sweating brow, frightened eyes. We notice these things as we read this psalm with all our senses on alert.

This is the prayer-psalm of an innocent person under extreme pressure. Attacked by ungodly enemies, he appeals to the Lord as Judge, begging him to attend and to 'see what is right' (*v. 2*). He declares his innocence of the lying claims that have been made against him. He declares his integrity, for he has been examined and tested, as metal is tested and refined. Both his words (*v. 3*) and his actions (*v. 4*) have been honest. He has avoided the way of the wicked; his feet have walked steadily in the tracks of God. In desperation he cries out to God for vindication.

The psalmist stands at a fixed point in history, a solitary figure in desperate need. As he lifts his head, he remembers the God of covenant love who delivered his people at the time of the exodus from Egypt. 'Do it again, Lord,' he cries. He prays for God's protection, 'as the apple of your eye' and 'in the shadow of your wings'. These images recall God's protective love for his covenant people in their desert wanderings (see *Deut 32:11*).

In strong, poetic language he then describes the wicked who pursue him. Like a lion that has tracked him down, the wicked are ready to pounce and tear him to pieces. He asks God to destroy them, just as he dealt with Pharaoh and his forces at the Red Sea.

In conclusion, the psalmist describes how blessed God's righteous ones are, and then expresses his own personal confidence and hope. It will soon no longer be the threatening enemies that he sees before him, but the very face of God, his comforting, reassuring presence.

To reflect on

I have a friend who ends her letters to me with this blessing from Psalm 17: 'May God keep you as the apple of his eye and hide you in the shadow of his wings.' Pass this blessing on to someone else today.

MONDAY 17 SEPTEMBER

Bright Morning Star

Isaiah 60:1–3

'I am the Root and the Offspring of David, and the bright Morning Star' (Rev 22:16, NIV).

Our alarm went off at 1.00 this morning. My husband and I pulled ourselves out of a deep sleep, put on warm dressing-gowns, then tip-toed outside to gaze up into the sky. An eclipse of the moon was taking place. It was unusual for the length of time it took to happen – one hour and forty-seven minutes. The experts tell us that the next lunar eclipse will be in seven years' time, but one of this morning's duration will not happen for another thousand years. That's why we had to see it!

As we gazed into the sky, I was awed by the unusually dark moon with its pink glow, and by the stars that were on full sparkling display. Thinking of Jesus, the bright Morning Star, made those stars seem even more glorious.

Stars are frequently mentioned in Scripture in connection with Jesus. The star of Numbers 24:17 is a direct prophecy of Jesus. Peter wrote about the morning star, that is, Jesus, rising in people's hearts (*2 Pet 1:19*). The morning star is one of the rewards promised to those who overcome (*Rev 2:28*).

The morning star, called 'son of the morning', heralds the dawning of the new day. Jesus, the Son of the Morning, heralds the arrival of the kingdom of God that is both already here and still coming. The morning star shines on even when obscured by mists or clouds. Similarly, nothing can stop God from his purposes, which are daily being fulfilled through Jesus. The morning star is a guiding light to those at sea. Jesus, the bright Morning Star, guides all who are lost or storm-tossed.

The story is told of a man trekking through a part of Africa with a group of local helpers. As night came the party set up camp and settled down to sleep. In the still darkness a word quietly passed from person to person – *Lutanda* ('morning star'). It was the word of agreement to be up and ready to move when the morning star appeared.

Welcome him today – Jesus – our bright Morning Star!

TUESDAY 18 SEPTEMBER

Man of Sorrows

Isaiah 52:13–53:12

'He was despised and rejected by men, a man of sorrows, and familiar with suffering. Like one from whom men hide their faces he was despised, and we esteemed him not' (53:3, NIV).

'Man of sorrows! What a name...' wrote songwriter Philip Bliss. What a name indeed! Did Mary know that in naming her baby 'Jesus', this other name stood like a dark shadow behind it? Did she know that he was born to die? Perhaps the gift of myrrh brought at his birth should have warned her of his pain and suffering that lay ahead. Was she familiar with Isaiah's song of the servant who would be despised, rejected, smitten, afflicted, pierced and crushed?

He grew from the root of Jesse. His beginnings were humble. Although he was of the royal line of David, there was nothing regal about his birth or his bearing, nothing that made him stand out from ordinary men. So he was easy to ignore or reject. He was like a lamb, meek, silent and defenceless, being led to the slaughterhouse. In Gethsemane as he faced the cross in anguish, his sweat was like drops of blood. On the cross, his side was pierced by a soldier's spear, bringing a flow of blood and water, proof that he was dead.

Onto the shoulders of this Man of Sorrows, God laid the sins of the world. This defenceless, sinless lamb was God's chosen sacrifice for the sins of all people for all time. His punishment would be the means of bringing us peace. 'Look, the Lamb of God, who takes away the sin of the world,' announced John when he saw Jesus coming towards him. He was a Man to be welcomed.

'Look,' said Pilate when Jesus stood before him, battered and bloodied. 'I find no reason to condemn this man.' He was a Man to be pardoned. 'Crucify him,' demanded the chief priests and their officials. The crowd took up the cry. He was a Man to be got rid of.

Jesus, the Man of Sorrows, stands before us today. This life-giving, sin-bearing Lamb of God asks for our verdict. Do we ignore him or invite him? Reject him or receive him?

To reflect on

Each rejection is a nail that crucifies him again.

WEDNESDAY 19 SEPTEMBER

Lion and Lamb

Revelation 5:1–10

' "See, the Lion of the tribe of Judah, the Root of David, has triumphed. He is able to open the scroll and its seven seals." Then I saw a Lamb' (vv. 5,6, NIV).

In his heavenly vision recorded in the book of Revelation, the apostle John sees a scroll that contains the full account of what God has in store for the world. The papyrus scroll has seven seals, indicating the importance of its contents. But, the angel asks, who is worthy to break the seals and open the scroll? John weeps in response. Then one of the elders tells him to dry his eyes and to look, for the Lion of the tribe of Judah is worthy. John looks but, instead of a Lion, he sees a Lamb. Jesus is pictured in these verses as both a lion (symbolising his authority and power) and a lamb (symbolising his submission to God's will).

As the Lamb, Jesus was the perfect sacrifice for the sins of all humanity. From the beginning of Scripture, the lamb holds a significant place. As a sacrificial animal, it had to be male, without blemish and of gentle nature. On the night of the Passover, the blood of the sacrificial lamb was sprinkled on the doorposts of the Israelite people, thus saving them from God's judgment.

On Mount Moriah Isaac called to his father Abraham, 'Where is the lamb?' and the question echoed across the ages and was answered by John the Baptist as he looked upon Jesus and declared, 'Look, the Lamb of God, who takes away the sin of the world!' (*John 1:29*).

As the Lion, Jesus came from the tribe of Judah whose banner bore a lion as their God-given symbol of strength and sovereignty (see *Gen 49:8–10*). In the final chapter of the world's story, Jesus will usher in his worldwide reign. Christ the Lion will be victorious because of what Christ the Lamb has done! Lamb and Lion – meekness and majesty, gentleness and glory, submission and strength!

To reflect on

C. S. Lewis had it right in his **Chronicles of Narnia** ***when he portrayed Aslan, the symbol of Jesus, as a lion. 'Is he safe?' asks Lucy. 'Course he isn't safe,' says Mr Beaver. 'But he's good. He's the King, I tell you.'***

THURSDAY 20 SEPTEMBER

Rock

1 Corinthians 10:1–13

'From the ends of the earth I call to you, I call as my heart grows faint; lead me to the rock that is higher than I' (Ps 61:2, NIV).

The picture of Jesus as a Rock is a powerful image, full of strength and solid reassurance. He is like a rock under our feet when the circumstances of life make us tremble. He is a secure rock of refuge when we need a place to shelter. With full hearts we sing, 'Rock of ages, cleft for me' and sense the strength of those words.

But the picture behind the rock is one of warning. In writing to the carnal Christians at Corinth, Paul used an example from the history of the Israelite people to warn them. The children of Israel had been saved from slavery in Egypt, led out by cloud and fire, the symbols of God's presence, then miraculously through the Red Sea and into a new life of freedom. Note how Paul repeats the word 'all' to emphasise the privilege of being the people whom God had delivered so dramatically. They were fed with manna that covered the ground like dew each morning, and with quail each evening (*Exod 16:12–13*). When they needed water, Moses struck the rock and water poured forth (*Exod 17:6*).

In their new place of freedom, however, their songs of deliverance quickly changed to sounds of grumbling and murmuring. Their stated intention to serve God alone turned to idolatry. They were a blessed and favoured people, yet tragically they held carelessly the divine provision and, as a result, all of that first generation to leave Egypt, except for Joshua and Caleb, died in the wilderness.

The rock from which the water came, and the manna, are symbolic of the supernatural sustenance that God continually provides for his people through Jesus, the water of life and the bread of life. Jesus is the Rock upon whom we stand, and from whom all blessings flow. Let us receive his blessings today with grateful, not careless hands.

He hideth my soul in the cleft of the rock
That shadows a dry, thirsty land;
He hideth my life in the depths of his love,
And covers me there with his hand.

***Fanny Crosby,* SASB 710**

FRIDAY 21 SEPTEMBER

Stone

1 Peter 2:4–10

'In Scripture it says: "See, I lay a stone in Zion, a chosen and precious cornerstone, and the one who trusts in him will never be put to shame" ' (v. 6, NIV).

There is a trail of stones winding its way through the Bible, not unlike the trail that Hansel in the children's story dropped behind him as he and his sister Gretel were led deep into the woods. The Bible trail is made up of some quite ordinary stones, as well as some very precious gems.

There are memorial stones, altars of remembrance, such as Jacob set up at Bethel. This 'house of God' had no home comforts, just a stone pillow that became a pillar with God's presence and blessing (*Gen 28:10–22*).

There is a heart of stone, which God promised to replace with a heart of flesh in all who believe (*Ezek 36:24–27*).

There are temptation stones, which may have looked like little loaves of bread, used by Satan to tempt Jesus at the end of his forty days and forty nights in the desert (*Matt 4:3*).

There are condemnation stones, picked up and ready to fling at the woman caught in adultery. Jesus bent down, not to pick up a stone, but to write something on the ground and thus avert his eyes. There was the slow thud of stones being dropped as her accusers walked away. When Jesus looked up at the woman his eyes spoke forgiveness (*John 8:1–11*).

There is the imperishable white stone with a new name on it, promised to believers who overcome in the fight of faith (*Rev 2:17*).

Towering above all these stones stands Jesus who is called a Living Stone, a precious stone for believers, but a stumbling-stone for those who reject him. Despised and rejected by those who discounted his claim to be Messiah, Jesus has become the Head Cornerstone, occupying the most important position in the building. Built into him, believers are built together like living stones into the very dwelling of God.

To reflect on

Find an ordinary stone today. Let it speak to you of Jesus, the Living Stone. Then let it become a memorial stone as you celebrate his work in your life.

SATURDAY 22 SEPTEMBER

Gift

John 4:1–15

'Jesus answered her, "If you knew the gift of God and who it is that asks you for a drink, you would have asked him and he would have given you living water" ' (v. 10, NIV).

With the opposition against him growing, Jesus left Jerusalem to travel north toward Galilee. Most Jews would have given Samaria a wide berth because of the mixed race of people who lived there. Jesus, however, chose not to live by such cultural restraints, and took the direct route, which brought him to the Samaritan town of Sychar. There at the village well he met a woman who had come in the heat of the day to draw water.

His conversation with her was a gift. In speaking to this woman, Jesus broke through cultural, and also social barriers. After all, she was foreign, female and fallen! Coming to the well at the noon hour kept her away from the comments and disdainful stares of the other women. For a man to speak to such a woman in a public place was unthinkable. But Jesus did. He knew her lonely present as well as her shady past.

He offered her another gift – living water. With her mind set on filling her water jug and returning home as quickly as possible, she was confused about the water of which he spoke. Living water instead of well water. It sounded great, especially if the supply he was talking about meant that her days of carrying water in the searing midday heat could cease. Her life would be a whole lot easier. But who was this man making such an outrageous offer? After all, only the Messiah could give living water that could forever quench one's deepest thirst.

In asking her for water, Jesus opened the way into her heart for the gift that he brought – namely himself. For this woman and for all who believe, Jesus comes as the gift of God, given as an expression of love (*John 3:16*), wrapped in humanity but full of divinity as well. 'Thanks be to God,' wrote Paul, 'for his indescribable gift!' (*2 Cor 9:15*).

To reflect on

Having received the Gift, our calling is to live to the glory of the Giver!

SUNDAY 23 SEPTEMBER

A Royal Thanksgiving

Psalm 18

'The LORD is my rock, my fortress and my deliverer; my God is my rock, in whom I take refuge. He is my shield and the horn of my salvation, my stronghold' (v. 2, NIV).

Psalm 18 is a magnificent hymn of praise to God, which begins with a deeply personal statement: 'I love you, O Lord.' This intimacy of relationship with God grew in the midst of the dangerous, life-threatening situations that the psalmist faced. King David may be speaking at a victory celebration after a series of campaigns, or he may be giving his 'retirement speech', the valedictory summing up of his life with God.

With great vigour and using strong, poetic imagery, he describes God as his rock, fortress, deliverer, refuge, shield, stronghold and horn of salvation. He lists the personal difficulties he faced. He was entangled by the cords of death, overwhelmed by the torrents of destruction, coiled around by the cords of the grave, confronted by the snares of death. Out of this distress he called to the Lord, and God responded fiercely. The earth trembled, the foundations of the mountains shook, smoke rose from his nostrils, fire from his mouth. He descended from the heavens covered in darkness, under a canopy of rain clouds, and mounted on cherubim. Hailstones and lightning rained destruction like arrows on the enemy, while an enormous blast of breath from God's nostrils parted the sea and laid bare the earth's foundations.

Suddenly the tone changes. The psalmist tells how God gently reached down with his own hand and pulled him from the deathly clutch of waters and enemies and placed him safely on a dry and spacious land. He then goes on to tell of what he did: 'I pursued, I overtook, I crushed.' But it is wrapped around with what God has done: 'He armed me with strength, he enabled me, he delivered me.'

This is the language of praise and prayer – rugged and real, grounded in the time and place of David's distress and deliverance. 'The Lord lives! Praise be to my Rock! Exalted be God my Saviour!' Having begun with a word of love, he concludes with a song of praise.

To reflect on

How would your song of praise to God sound?

MONDAY 24 SEPTEMBER

Bread

John 6:25–35

'Then Jesus declared, "I am the bread of life. He who comes to me will never go hungry, and he who believes in me will never be thirsty" ' (v. 35, NIV).

When Moses asked God in the desert of Midian, 'Who are you?' he replied, 'I AM WHO I AM' (*Exod 3:14*). When Jesus' followers puzzled as to his identity, he responded in a similar way. 'I am the bread of life' was the first of seven descriptions of himself that he gave.

For many people today, bread is just an item on the shopping list, to be bought at the supermarket – sliced, gluten-free, herb, enriched, wholemeal, super-white or however you like it. It's common and everyday and not at all special.

Change the setting to a place of necessity, however, and bread takes on a new meaning. At Chikankata, Zambia, the bread that was brought in from nearby Mazabuka each week on the delivery truck was often on the brink of turning blue! I soon learned how to make bread, and the task became a holy act. The respectful handling, the patient waiting and then the glorious aroma of the baking bread all spoke warmth and welcome.

Change the setting again to another place of necessity and recall the manna that God sent to feed the hungry Israelite people in the desert after their escape from Egypt. With that heavenly bread, Moses had fed a whole nation. There was a popular Jewish expectation that when the Messiah came he would once again send manna from heaven. But when Jesus declared himself the 'bread that came down from heaven' (*v. 41*), the people were slow to understand. After all, unlike Moses, Jesus had fed only 5,000, and that was with quite ordinary bread.

Jesus pointed out that it was not Moses who had given them manna in the desert, but God. He lifted their eyes from manna to a man, from their stomachs to Someone, living bread, life-giving bread.

To reflect on

Jesus did not call himself the fruit cake or the chocolate pudding of life, but the bread of life. He is our necessary, welcoming, nourishing, sustaining, aromatic, broken and freely offered bread, for all who will come and believe (see v. 35).

TUESDAY 25 SEPTEMBER

Light

John 9:1–12

'When Jesus spoke again to the people, he said, "I am the light of the world. Whoever follows me will never walk in darkness, but will have the light of life" ' (8:12, NIV).

When the devout old man Simeon took the young baby Jesus in his arms in the temple, he knew this was no ordinary child (*Luke 2:28*). Having been promised that he would not die until he had seen the Messiah, Simeon recognised this baby as the salvation of God. This child, he said, is 'a God-revealing light to the non-Jewish nations, and of glory for your people Israel' (*v. 32, The Message*).

The title 'Light' is one that shines upon Jesus especially through the Gospel of John, where the word is used time and time again to describe him and his mission. Just as light is shown most clearly when it pierces the darkness, so Jesus, as the light that came from God, shines most clearly when his words and actions are seen against a dark background.

In chapter 8, John tells the story of the woman caught in adultery who was brought before Jesus. Ignoring the Pharisees' demands that she be stoned for her sin, Jesus extends forgiveness and sets her free. In chapter 9, he heals a man who has been blind from birth. The Pharisees look for someone to blame for the man's affliction and then turn their anger upon Jesus for healing the man on the Sabbath. Between these two incidents, Jesus does battle with the religious leaders, answering their questions, turning their words back upon themselves and challenging them to face the truth that stands in person before their very eyes. These incidents happened during the Feast of Tabernacles (see *7:2*) when the blaze from the great temple candelabra lit up every corner of Jerusalem. 'This light shines for a time,' he says, 'but the light I offer will last for ever.'

To a woman with a sinful past, he offered a life-giving word. To a man born blind, he offered a light-giving word. To a people blinded by prejudice, darkened in their understanding and refusing to hear and accept the truth, Jesus held out both life and light. The same offer is extended to us today.

Today

Receive his light! Reflect his light!

WEDNESDAY 26 SEPTEMBER

Shepherd

John 10:1–18

'I am the good shepherd; I know my sheep and my sheep know me . . . and I lay down my life for the sheep' (vv. 14,15, NIV).

I grew up in the lush open spaces of sheep-farming country in the south of New Zealand. Every summer a shearing gang would move in for a couple of weeks. These good-hearted, fun-loving workers were full of energy and practical jokes. They wore black singlets, and the lanolin from the sheep's wool made their skin shine. They had voracious appetites and consumed three cooked meals a day, plus extras. My mother would be exhausted by the time they left and she couldn't face food for about a fortnight afterwards.

The biblical picture of a shepherd is a long way from these rugged workers. The land of Palestine was rough and stony pastoral country. There were no closed paddocks, and sheep grazed everywhere under the watchful eye of a shepherd. His task was to keep the flock together and to guard them against predators. At night, if the sheep were near a village they would be sheltered in a communal sheepfold along with other flocks. In the morning, each shepherd would call his own flock out in a sing-song language that the sheep recognised. If the sheep were out on the hills they would be gathered into an enclosed area and the shepherd would lie across the opening, thus becoming the door to the sheepfold. During the day he would go ahead of the flock in search of new pasture and to make sure the track was safe. Being kept for their wool, the sheep would often be under the care of the same shepherd for many years. He would call them by pet names, watch over them in the lambing season, become familiar with their ways.

The parallels are clear. To a people familiar with the role and person of the shepherd, Jesus said, 'I am the good shepherd. As shepherds care for their sheep, so I care for the people who follow me. I guard this flock, I lead them to safe pasture, I know them. My voice is one they know and can trust. It is always a voice of love.'

Prayer

Saviour, like a Shepherd lead me.

THURSDAY 27 SEPTEMBER

Resurrection and Life

John 11:1–27

'Jesus said to her, "I am the resurrection and the life. He who believes in me will live, even though he dies; and whoever lives and believes in me will never die. Do you believe this?" ' (vv. 25,26, NIV).

What an amazing week that was! Lazarus wasn't well. He had caught a cold and the hot lemon drinks and barley soup I made didn't seem to help. Then it settled on his chest and in no time he had a hacking cough. Within a couple of days he was feverish. Mary didn't seem concerned. She just sat and sang her songs. But I felt alarm rising within me as the hours went by and he showed no sign of improvement.

Eventually, I knew I had to do something and I told Mary I was going to call a doctor. 'Oh, why?' she asked. 'Why don't you just call the Master? He'll come when he knows his dear friend is sick.' For once, the girl spoke sense! So we sent a message to Jesus. I kept looking for him. After all, this was an emergency.

The messenger had no sooner gone than Lazarus lost all strength. With every cough he got weaker. The next morning, after a very restless night, he had a huge coughing fit, then suddenly all was quiet, and I knew it was all over. It was too late for Jesus. I felt so sad about my brother, but even sadder that his friend had not come in time.

A full four days – four days! – passed before we heard that he was on his way. By then, sorrow had knocked all the fight out of me, but I went out to welcome him.

'Jesus,' I blurted out, 'Jesus, if you had been here, my brother would not have died! But,' I added rather weakly, 'even now I know you can bring him back to life again.'

'He will rise again,' said Jesus.

'Oh yes, Lord, I know the doctrine of resurrection at the end of time.'

'No, Martha,' said Jesus, taking hold of my hands. 'You don't have to wait until then. I'm not talking doctrine. Look at me, Martha. I am resurrection and life! Death cannot hold onto anyone who believes in me. Your brother will live. Come, let me show you what I mean.'

FRIDAY 28 SEPTEMBER

Vine

John 15:1–17

'Remain in me, and I will remain in you. No branch can bear fruit by itself; it must remain in the vine. Neither can you bear fruit unless you remain in me' (v. 4, NIV).

When my husband and I moved to our present quarters, we were delighted to find a grapevine growing along the garden fence. It looked in need of some nurture, however, so we enquired as to how to 'feed' a grapevine. 'The best way,' said a farmer, 'is to bury half a dead sheep underneath it, because a grapevine is a meat-eater.' Half a dead sheep proved rather difficult to find and the neighbour's cat looked very healthy, but we did find a rich source of freshly slaughtered meat – dead possums on nearby quiet country roads! Since then the grapevine has flourished, producing an annual harvest of sweet and juicy grapes.

In his last 'I am' statement, Jesus calls himself the true vine. The image may have been prompted by the wine at the table, or the impending shadow of Gethsemane with its olive trees, or the vine symbol carved on the porch of the Temple. Certainly it would be familiar to those who heard him speak. In declaring himself the true (that is, genuine) vine, Jesus was comparing himself with Israel, the fruitless vine, of whom God said 'he looked for a crop of good grapes, but it yielded only bad fruit' (*Isa 5:2*).

Anyone who tends a vine knows that the pruning process is vital to the healthy growth of the plant. Just as the branches are cut back to secure the growth of the fruit, so the qualities of character (*Gal 5:22,23*) and fruits such as answered prayer (*v. 7*), joy (*v. 11*) and love (*v. 12*) grow out of the daily discipline of living in Jesus.

The word 'remain' is repeated over and over again. 'Remain in me . . .' 'Remain in the vine . . .' 'Remain in my love . . .' Just as a branch cut off from the main vine has no life in itself, so a believer has no life or fruitfulness when severed from union and fellowship with Jesus.

To reflect on

Apart from him we are nothing, but in him we can do everything! That's God's promise. (Phil 1:11; 4:13)

SATURDAY 29 SEPTEMBER

KING OF KINGS AND LORD OF LORDS

Revelation 19:11–16

'On his robe and on his thigh he has this name written: KING OF KINGS AND LORD OF LORDS' (v. 16, NIV).

While many of the names of Jesus, such as bread, stone, or vine, have a familiar, everyday picture behind them, this last name, KING OF KINGS AND LORD OF LORDS, lifts us from the familiar present to a future day when Jesus will come to rule the world (*Rev 11:15*).

The wise men who came looking for him at his birth adored him as king. 'Where is the one who has been born king of the Jews?' they asked. 'We saw his star in the east and have come to worship him' (*Matt 2:2*). He was born a king because he was a king before he was born (*John 18:37*).

The people who welcomed him as he rode into Jerusalem acclaimed him as king (*Matt 21:5*). Unlike a military conqueror, this king came in humility and peace, riding on a donkey. The people cried out their Hosanna welcome and spread cloaks and branches on the road in an act of homage.

Pilate had a placard prepared for the cross, which acknowledged Jesus as king. 'It read: JESUS OF NAZARETH, THE KING OF THE JEWS' (*John 19:19*). The crime for which he was executed was just that – being the king of the Jews. The 'chief priests of the Jews' (*v. 21*) – note the contrast – were appalled that he should be given such a title.

In Revelation, the picture is complete. When Jesus reveals himself as the King of Kings and Lord of Lords, his reign in righteousness will be universally acknowledged. All other kings and lesser rulers will be under his control. Then 'every knee should bow . . . and every tongue confess that Jesus Christ is Lord, to the glory of God the Father' (*Phil 2:10,11*).

The servant becomes the Saviour. The one crowned with thorns will be crowned with glory. Accept this King and give him your allegiance today!

King of Kings and Lord of Lords,
Glory, Hallelujah!
Jesus, Prince of Peace,
Glory, Hallelujah!

Sophie Conty/Naomi Batya[4]

SUNDAY 30 SEPTEMBER

A Sunrise Hymn

Psalm 19

'The heavens declare the glory of God; the skies proclaim the work of his hands' (v. 1, NIV).

Psalm 19 has been called 'the greatest poem in the Psalter and one of the greatest lyrics in the world' (C. S. Lewis, *Reflections on the Psalms*). It is both beautiful poetry and profound theology.

The psalmist moves in dramatic way from macrocosm to microcosm, from the universe and its glory to the individual in humility before God. He begins by reflecting on God's revelation in nature. Silently, wordlessly, the heavens give dramatic testimony to God's existence, his power and his orderliness. The heavens are the divinely pitched tent for the sun, the supreme metaphor for the glory of God, as it makes its daily triumphant sweep across the world. 'Nothing is hidden from its heat', that is, from God's presence.

As the sun dominates the daytime sky, so too does the law of God dominate human life. Just as there can be no life without the sun, so there can be no true life without the revealed word of God. Nothing is hidden from its penetrating gaze. In every way the law of God is good – it is perfect, sure, upright, pure, radiant and true. It is indeed a light to our path (*Ps 119:105*). It is even more desirable than fine gold and sweet honey, the objects of much human striving.

Suddenly aware of his own insignificance and unworthiness, the psalmist asks for forgiveness and deliverance from great transgression, hidden faults and open rebellion. Having seen the greatness of God in his created world, and the holiness of God in his written word, the psalmist sees his own sinfulness in stark relief.

The last verse brings together the themes of praise and prayer. The heavens praise God by their very existence. The psalmist too wishes to join that cosmic chorus of praise, right down to the way he speaks and thinks. These words are the psalmist's prayer, the preacher's prayer, the author's prayer.

Let this verse be your prayer today: 'May the words of my mouth and the meditation of my heart be pleasing in your sight, O Lord, my Rock and my Redeemer.'

A LIFE OF PRAYER

Introduction

A sign on the back of a car sent me once again exploring how prayer works and what God does with it. The sign read, 'Pray to stop abortion'. I wondered – do we need to convince God that abortion is wrong? Do we need to plead with him to stop something that is contrary to his will? Does this really change the heart of God that has been fixed on humankind in fierce and abiding love from the beginning?

Certainly he needs no such reminder. God knows what we need even before we ask. Yet, we are instructed to pray – without ceasing. Why do we find that so hard? Certainly how we pray is guided by what we believe and how we perceive God. Is prayer rigorous discipline or required spiritual exercise? Why can we not view it as simply keeping company with God?

Perhaps we pray so little because we live in a world that scoffs at God and debunks the saints. We live in a time when many have moved the locus of morality from an external to an internal source. But unless modern thinkers can locate a source of moral authority somewhere else than in the collective sentiments of human beings, we will always be vulnerable to dangerous swings of moral consensus.

The dangerous climate in our world today affects all Christians. We believe that human society was meant to be a covenant between God and humankind, a collaborative enterprise based on common values and vision. But we are blown by prevailing winds, and only a dedicated, determined will to persevere in fellowship with God and his saints will keep us morally upright in the cyclonic rage of agnostic, immoral pressures.

God designed our lives to be a covenant between himself and humanity. We keep our terms of the covenant through fellowship with him in prayer. And what is the goal of our covenant keeping? 'When Christ, who is your life, appears, then you also will appear with him in glory' (*Col 3:4*).

Lt-Col Marlene Chase
National Editor-in-Chief, USA

MONDAY 1 OCTOBER

The Lifeline

Matthew 6:5–14

'Let the word of Christ dwell in you richly as you teach and admonish one another with all wisdom, and as you sing psalms, hymns and spiritual songs with gratitude in your hearts to God' (Col 3:16, NIV).

To know and love God – this is the object of both life and prayer. Nothing is more important; nothing has more challenged my own heart throughout over thirty-five years of service. And I am more penitent for prayerlessness than for any other omission in my life.

From its beginning, The Salvation Army has placed consistent emphasis on prayer. William Booth, who in 1903 was invited to open the United States Senate with an invocation to God, urged Salvationists to 'pray believingly, live holily, labour earnestly'. He added, 'Then success in winning souls is certain.' Only prayer will bring success in holy living and winning souls. If we have neglected our prayer life, it's time to consider again that Jesus, who taught his disciples to pray, could not go a day without meeting his Father in fervent, loving prayer. And we must ask ourselves why he, who needed to pray so little, prayed so much when we, who need to pray so much, pray so little.

Because our grasp on prayer has slipped, we must not refuse this lifeline when it is given. It is our life as well as 'our watchword at the gates of death' (Montgomery). We keep the terms of our life covenant with God through communion with him. We'll die without him as millions of the prayerless are dying today.

We begin our focus on this vital communion with adoration of our Holy God who desires that we too become holy. Those who would live a holy life will be tempted at every turn to give up. But, 'The one who calls you is faithful and he will do it' (*1 Thess 5:24*). 'Holiness is but the unfolding of Christ's own character in the life of the believer,' said Frederick Coutts. 'The more we open ourselves through study and prayer, the more we see the character of Christ unfolding and are able to let that character grow richly within us.' That is the reason for prayer. It is the cry of our souls made in his image and it is the desperate need of our age.

TUESDAY 2 OCTOBER

The Good and the Best

Matthew 7:7–12

Which of you, if his son asks for bread, will give him a stone? Or if he asks for a fish, will give him a snake? If you, then, though you are evil, know how to give good gifts to your children, how much more will your Father in heaven give good gifts to those who ask him!' (v. 9, NIV).

Tony Campolo, a well-known educator and author, recalls his young son announcing one evening, 'I'm going to pray now. Anybody want anything?' God longs to give us good things, but he created us for the best gift – fellowship with himself. To love God and to enjoy him forever – that's what a lifetime is for. But why should a holy God care whether we talk to him or not? Why should he want to be around us, snivelling, vacillating, unholy creatures that we are?

David wondered about this too. 'What is man that you are mindful of him?' (*Ps 8:4*). But God's word tells us that he has set his love upon us forever. We cultivate that fellowship through prayer. Prayer is friendship with God, a glowing, living, eternal fellowship.

Henri Nouwen tells of three monks who regularly visited St Anthony, the father of monks. Two discussed their thoughts and the salvation of their souls with him, but a third remained silent and did not ask him anything. 'You often come here to see me, but you never ask me anything,' noted St Anthony. The man replied, 'It is enough to see you, Father.'

Is it enough for us to see the Father? To be with him? Or are we blinded by our wants, deafened by the sound of our own appetites? The truth that God desires our fellowship should bring us to our knees. It should remind us that we are completely dependent upon him for life and sustenance. We could not live one day without him. This moves us to the essential element of prayer – adoration. Adoration is the spontaneous yearning of the heart to worship, honour, magnify and bless God. We are drawn by some inner restlessness, by some great emptiness that longs for God. And God, knowing that we are longing for him, gives us a sense of himself. That is the beginning of prayer – a longing for God. So we see that even our adoration of him is a gift.

'Your Father in heaven [will] give good gifts to those who ask him!'

WEDNESDAY 3 OCTOBER

'Come Let Us Adore Him'

Colossians 3:1–14

'Always giving thanks to God the Father for everything, in the name of our Lord Jesus Christ' (Eph 5:20, NIV).

Thanksgiving and praise weave in and out of one another and become part of a whole. Biblical writers frequently use the words interchangeably and even on top of one another: 'I will thank thee in the great congregation; in the mighty throng I will praise thee' (*Ps 35:18, RSV*). The Old Testament world was soaked with the language of thanksgiving. David chose certain priests to be ministers before the Ark of the Covenant with a singular commission, 'to invoke, thank and praise the Lord'. It's hard to find a page of the Psalter that doesn't contain the rhetoric of thanksgiving: 'O give thanks to the LORD, for he is good; for his steadfast love endures for ever!' (*Ps 106:1, RSV*).

Jesus was the premier example of gratitude. The signature written across his life was the prayer, 'I thank thee, Father, Lord of heaven and earth' (*Luke 10:21, RSV*). Paul, too, wrote, 'I thank my God through Jesus Christ for all of you' (*Rom 1:8*), and lived a life of deep gratitude. Praise lies on a higher plane than thanksgiving. When we give thanks, our thoughts still circle about ourselves to some extent. But in praise our souls ascend to self-forgetting adoration, praising only the majesty of God. The writer to the Hebrews urges us to 'continually offer up a sacrifice of praise to God' (*Heb 13:15, RSV*).

When we think of who God is and what he has done, it cannot but move us to astonishment, then to thanksgiving, then to praise. Yet, in spite of his greatness, he cares about communion with us. He wants us to long for him even as he longs for us to communicate with him, to enjoy him.

'Our God is not made of stone. His heart is the most sensitive and tender of all,' writes Richard Foster. 'No act goes unnoticed, no matter how insignificant. A cup of cold water is enough to put tears in the eyes of God. Like the mother who delights to receive a wilted bouquet of dandelions from her child, so God celebrates our feeble expressions of gratitude.'

THURSDAY 4 OCTOBER

Children of Prayer

Luke 10:21–24

'I praise you, Father, Lord of heaven and earth, because you have hidden these things from the wise and learned, and revealed them to little children. Yes, Father, for this was your good pleasure' (v. 21, NIV).

Now as always, God discloses himself to 'babes' and hides himself in thick darkness from the wise and prudent. We must simplify our approach to him. We must strip down to essentials (and they will be found to be blessedly few). We must put away all effort to impress, and come with the guileless candour of childhood. If we do this, without doubt God will quickly respond.

A.W. Tozer, *The Pursuit of God*

God wants us to come to him as children come to their parents (*Luke 11:11–13*), knowing that God gives what is good. Jesus taught us to pray so that we wouldn't succumb to temptation, even as he drew personal strength to face crucifixion and death (*Luke 22:39–46*).

As God's children, we come to him with a loving heart. We press in toward the divine centre where we learn who he is. Mother Teresa said, 'It is not what we say but what God says to us and through us. All our words are useless if they do not come from within. Words that do not carry the light of Christ only increase the darkness.'

As loved children we come to him in earnest faith. 'Apart from me you can do nothing,' Jesus said (*John 15:5*). Without prayer we may build buildings, alleviate physical hunger, produce amazing literature, but we will do nothing of permanence. This is true because prayer puts us in communication not with techniques but with the Teacher. There is too little hunger for union with Christ in our prayers. And oneness with Christ is after all the greatest result of continuous, believing prayer.

We come like children in complete dependence. We need consciously to appropriate his grace every moment, every day. God wants us to ask, not because he loves to hear us beg, but because he knows we have short memories and often forget that he is the One who supplies our needs.

These attitudes – humility, a loving heart, an earnest faith and complete dependence – are necessary if we are to touch God in prayer and have fellowship with him.

FRIDAY 5 OCTOBER

The Prayer of the Humble Heart

Luke 18:9–14

'The sacrifices of God are a broken spirit; a broken and contrite heart, O God, you will not despise' (Ps 51:17, NIV).

'At the beginning of all spiritual endeavour stands humility,' notes Fredrich Dessauer, an atomic physicist. 'And he who loses it can achieve no other heights than the heights of disillusionment.' Christ taught humility through example and precept during his sojourn on earth and urged his disciples to express this grace in every area of their lives, especially in the discipline of prayer.

It should always be in the deepest spirit of humility that we approach God. We can learn much about prayer from his Word and from putting into practice the elements of prayer, but we must accept that communion with our Creator is mystery. We simply cannot put God in any kind of box and know precisely how he operates. If we could, we would not have any need or desire to worship him.

The psalmist says in desperation, 'His ways are past finding out!' Yet, we are told to 'seek the Lord', to 'be still and know who he is'. The apostle Paul speaks often of mystery – the mystery of God and his Church likened to a bride and bridegroom, the mystery of treasure in earthen vessels, the mystery of the resurrection. In Colossians 1:27 he speaks of, 'the riches of the glory of this mystery, which is Christ in you, the hope of Glory' (*RSV*).

That God desires our company mystifies us, amazes us, brings us to our knees as we recognise how sinful we are. Like Isaiah, we find ourselves naked before him, realising we have no good thing to commend ourselves. We bow before him, the God of the universe who spoke whole worlds into existence. He calls us into the mystery, into himself.

This attitude of humility does not contradict the invitation to 'come boldly before the throne of grace'. Because Jesus Christ tore down the veil that separated sinful man from holy God, we can come as his loved children, but as humble children who recognise who God is. As Pascal put it, 'Jesus Christ is a God whom we approach without pride, and before whom we humble ourselves without despair.'

SATURDAY 6 OCTOBER

Prayer is for Lovers

John 15:1–15

'As the Father has loved me, so have I loved you. Now remain in my love . . . If you remain in me and my words remain in you, ask whatever you wish, and it will be given you' (vv. 9,7, NIV).

When we are in prayer, we are in touch with Love. God calls us to himself because he longs to have fellowship with us. Praying is keeping company with God. It is a communion of lovers, a pressing in toward the divine centre from which all of life emanates and around which everything progresses and holds together. From the very beginning, when he sought Adam in the cool of the garden, God established communication with himself. We read that, 'the LORD used to speak to Moses face to face, as a man speaks to his friend' (*Exod 33:11, RSV*).

Hebrew believers included God in every detail of their lives. They carried on conversations about the daily stuff of living. Though their prayers were sometimes self-centred, they learned 'other-centredness' through the reality of simple prayer. 'I am always with you,' wrote the psalmist. 'You hold me by my right hand. You guide me with your counsel, and afterwards you will take me into glory' (*Ps 73:23,24*).

Jesus spoke of prayer as 'remaining in the Father's love' (*John 15*) through constant communication. We read that he rose early, a long time before it was day, or went off to a lonely place to pray. He taught us that it is impossible to stay connected to God without prayer. It is impossible to do what is right without his help through prayer. Unaided we will fail miserably because we are sinful by nature, and we are surrounded by other sinners. We will find it impossible to stand for right when those around us are standing for evil, unless God helps us!

It is impossible to love God and others without prayer. Jesus depended on his Father in a rich, continuous relationship. Far from our habit of 'saying our prayers' in times of stress and difficulty, Jesus' relationship with God was permanent and sustained. He wasn't even in the habit of having only frequent time alone with God, but his was a way of life, continual and deep, which flowed out of his life in love for all humankind.

SUNDAY 7 OCTOBER

Preparing for Battle

Psalm 20

'Some trust in chariots and some in horses, but we trust in the name of the LORD our God' (v. 7, NIV).

Warfare was an inevitable part of the landscape in ancient Israel. The difference between Israel and her warring neighbours, however, was the presence of a Warrior God who fought the battles with his people (*Exod 15:3*).

In Psalm 20 it seems that a battle or military campaign is about to begin. From a military point of view, such a battle required careful planning, well-trained troops, superior military resources to those of the enemy, and the courage to fight. But something else was required before the departure. The people knew that success in battle depended primarily on God, not on their military planning and strategy.

A military campaign would thus commence in the Temple. The king, who both led the army and was the representative of God among the people, did not demand divine aid as a royal right. Rather he offered sacrifices to God, indicating both his unworthiness before God, and his desperate need of God's assistance. The sacrifice was a royal act, but the worship of which it was a part involved all the people. As he sacrificed, they expressed their prayer of petition and blessing. Everyone joined in his acknowledgement of unworthiness and prayer for assistance; everyone shared in the joyful anticipation of victory. After all, victory for him meant victory for them!

This twofold preparation for battle meant that the army went out well prepared with military resources, as well as acknowledging that lasting victory could not possibly come from those resources alone. The enemy would go forward boasting in the power of their military might, but God's people would go forward, confident in 'the name of the LORD' (*v. 7*). The enemy, now standing in their arrogance and might, would bow down and fall, whereas the king and his people, now bowed down in worship, would rise up in victory (*v. 8*).

We are a long way from ancient Israel in this day, but is there in Psalm 20 a pattern for the battles we face as Christians?

Prepare as if it all depends on you, and pray as if it all depends on God!

MONDAY 8 OCTOBER

Praying for One Another

1 Timothy 2:1–8

'Justice is turned back, and righteousness stands afar off; for truth has fallen in the public squares, and uprightness cannot enter. Truth is lacking, and he who departs from evil makes himself a prey. The LORD saw it, and it displeased him that there was no justice. He saw that there was . . . no one to intervene' (Isa 59:14–16, RSV).

Another translation says that God 'wondered that there was no intercessor'. I wonder how often I have given God cause to wonder about my reticence to intercede for another? Scripture teaches that 'supplications, prayers, intercessions, and thanksgivings be made for all men' (*1 Tim 2:1, RSV*).

What can we do if the desire to pray for others is simply not there? There may be many causes for this lack, but couldn't we begin by praying for an increase in our love for others? As God helps us grow in our capacity to care, we'll begin working for the good of our neighbours, friends and even enemies. We'll discover quickly that we can do little for them on our own. We'll be driven to seek God on their behalf. We'll want them to enter into things and receive things that we cannot give.

Intercessory prayer binds us together in community, keeps us from evil, and moves us toward Christian action. Let's not give God cause to wonder about our lack of intercession. Let's participate in the act of creating new persons in Christ, creating wholeness where there is sickness, understanding where there is dissension.

We do not need to understand how intercessory prayer works. We need only to pray for one another in obedience and love. A compelling prayer written by Søren Kierkegaard, nineteenth-century theologian and author, affirms this truth:

> Teach me, Lord, that the fight of faith is not a fight with doubt, thought against thought, but a fight for character. Enable me to see that human vanity consists in having to understand. Save me from the vanity of not being willing to obey like a child, and of wanting to be like a grown man who has to understand. Help me to realise that he who will not obey when he cannot understand does not, in any essential sense, obey you at all. Make me a believer, a 'character man', who, unreservedly obedient, sees it as necessary for his character's sake that he must not always understand. Make me willing to believe even when I cannot understand.

TUESDAY 9 OCTOBER

Prayer that Moves beyond the Miracle

John 4:43–53

'Though he slay me, yet will I hope in him . . . But he knows the way that I take; when he has tested me, I shall come forth as gold' (Job 13:15; 23:10, NIV).

When my sister passed away at the age of thirty-nine, my brother-in-law, who had been a minister for ten years, turned his back on God. He could no longer believe in a God who would cut off this woman whom he loved and who had so much to offer the world. No one blamed him for his anguish at being left to raise three school-age children alone. But Jim had not really believed in God as the loving and just Creator. He believed in a God who performed miracles along the lines of human justice and understanding.

Jim was not unlike the early Galileans who, though Jesus was raised among them, had no real faith in him. Theirs was a shallow, miracle-oriented faith, which failed to honour Jesus. In John's account, we see the father must have had a certain confidence in Jesus' ability to heal his son. But the man's faith had limits. Jesus would have to travel to the bedside of the boy if his healing power were to be effective. Further, if his son died, Jesus could have no further power to heal.

Jesus didn't rebuke the man's elementary faith but tested it, seeking to raise it to a higher level. Instead of going with him to Capernaum, Jesus told the father to return home alone, trusting in Jesus' simple assertion, 'Your son will live' (*v. 50*). This demanded a higher level of trust in Jesus than the man had known, but he took up the challenge and discovered that Jesus had healed his son long-distance!

Jesus still seeks to move us beyond limited faith to trust, even when we don't receive the answer we want. God still looks for people like Job whose faith doesn't depend on longed-for miracles.

What have you asked God for today? Does your faith allow God to work out his will for you even if it does not line up with your dreams? He wills only your very best. Faith, which is his gift to you, will grow in you daily as you seek his face and heart in prayer.

WEDNESDAY 10 OCTOBER

Praying in the Name of Jesus

Matthew 26:36–45

'I will raise up for myself a faithful priest, who shall do according to what is in my heart and in my mind; and I will build him a sure house, and he shall go in and out before my anointed for ever' (1 Sam 2:35, RSV).

We close our prayers with the words 'in Jesus' name'. For some it becomes a kind of superstitious formula, but to pray 'in the name of Jesus' involves praying in the spirit of Jesus, for the things that he purposes. When we pray in his name, we are praying for what he wills. We must not set our agenda and then ask him to follow. 'You did not choose me, but I chose you and appointed you to go and bear fruit – fruit that will last' (*John 15:16*).

Chiune Sugihara, a Japanese Christian living in Poland, had a dream to become his country's ambassador to Russia. He studied hard and steadily began his climb up the bureaucratic ladder. In the summer of 1940, Chiune woke up to find a group of Jews surrounding his house. They were desperate to escape Poland as Hitler's army encroached. Chiune was their only chance to avoid the death camps. They needed him to issue visas, allowing them to flee to freedom.

But the Japanese government had aligned itself with Hitler. And Sugihara would have to risk everything for the sake of these strangers. He wrote visa after visa, shoving them through train windows into the hands of desperate Jews. At night his wife massaged the cramps from his fingers. Sugihara never realised his lifelong dream to be an ambassador to Russia, but 10,000 Jews and their 40,000 descendants were saved from extermination because Chiune allowed God's plan to be fulfilled in his life. God had given him a greater ambassadorship.

No dream, however sweet, can compare with the sweet will of God. Praying in the name of Jesus means praying in the name and spirit of Jesus. That is why his pattern for us includes, 'Your will be done on earth as it is in heaven.' Until we are willing to will what he wills, we shall never be effective in prayer – either for our own souls or for others. And we shall never become the people of character and destiny he has planned for us.

THURSDAY 11 OCTOBER

Persistence in Prayer

1 Thessalonians 5:14–25

'And pray in the Spirit on all occasions with all kinds of prayers and requests. With this in mind, be alert and always keep on praying for all the saints' (Eph 6:18, NIV).

'Men ought always to pray and not to faint,' Scripture tells us. The inference is clear. If we do not pray and continue to pray through every day and in every experience, we will lose ground spiritually. We will become unconscious, unaffected by God's voice and leading. It is not always easy to continue in prayer when we don't see the answer to our prayers, or when the answer that comes disappoints us. 'But we will reap,' the Bible reminds us, 'if we don't give up!'

We learn something about persevering prayer following Elijah's confrontation with the prophets of Baal on Mount Carmel. It involves one weary servant who stayed by Elijah after the crowds had gone home (*1 Kgs 18:41–46*). Elijah had proved the sovereignty of God over the prophets of Baal. He told Ahab to go, eat and drink, for there was a sound of the rushing of rain.

Kneeling with his face between his knees, Elijah prayed for rain, the rain that God had withheld because of the wickedness of the people. Elijah suddenly called out to his servant to go up the steep rocky trail at the base of the mountain and look toward the sea. Seven times Elijah ordered the servant up the hill to look for rain. Seven times the servant patiently plodded up the path. That seventh time, a cloud as small as a man's hand appeared in the sky. Rain was coming. 'I see a cloud about the size of a man's hand,' the servant reported. It took seven trips before the servant got a glimpse of answered prayer.

We're often like that servant in our own prayer life. We don't mind going up the steep rocky path of prayer once, maybe twice, but that's all. We resist going back again. God has commanded persevering prayer. His answer may not come according to our timetable, but prayer keeps us alive in Christ and growing daily. Perseverance is needed for our own sanctification and for others who will be brought into the family of God.

FRIDAY 12 OCTOBER

Delayed Responses to Prayer

Luke 18:1–8

'So I say to you: Ask and it will be given to you; seek and you will find; knock and the door will be opened to you. For everyone who asks receives; he who seeks finds; and to him who knocks, the door will be opened' (Luke 11:9–10, NIV).

God wants humble and earnest asking, seeking, knocking. The very act of persisting in prayer helps us learn to praise him as sovereign Lord, not regard him as a divine vending machine.

The judge in Luke's parable was a godless person. What could he have in common with God who longs to give good gifts to his children? It was the judge's choice in each case to delay a response, out of selfish indifference. But God delays his responses out of love for he knows the end from the beginning. If God wants to answer our prayers and loves us with infinite love, we must concede that there could be reasons why God sometimes delays his answers.

We may need to deal with parts of our lives that are displeasing to God. The Bible records more than fifty times when God didn't answer someone's prayer and most were due to sin. Consider Saul who took charge of the battle offering wrongfully (it was the place of the priest) and who also sought counsel from a medium. In consequence of his disobedience, Saul's prayers were blocked. David declared, 'If I had cherished sin in my heart, the Lord would not have listened' (*Ps 66:18*).

Jesus told us that we should not pray if we have unresolved conflict with someone (*Mark 11:25*). James 4:3 pinpoints self-indulgence as a barrier: 'When you ask, you do not receive, because you ask with wrong motives, that you may spend what you get on your pleasures.' Husbands who dishonour their wives and vice versa will be hindered in prayer according to 1 Peter 3:7: 'Husbands, in the same way be considerate as you live with your wives . . . as heirs with you of the gracious gift of life, so that nothing will hinder your prayers.'

Self-examination is an important discipline in the life of the Christian. How does our practice line up with the precepts of his Word? Perhaps confession is in order before we appeal to the Lord. 'If you do what is right, will you not be accepted? But if you do not do what is right, sin is crouching at your door' (*Gen. 4:7*).

SATURDAY 13 OCTOBER

Growing in Christ

2 Peter 3:11–18

'But grow in the grace and knowledge of our Lord and Saviour Jesus Christ. To him be glory both now and for ever! Amen' (v. 18, NIV).

Delayed responses from God do not always signal some act of disobedience or omission. God may be waiting for growth in our lives before he answers. Habakkuk couldn't understand why God was punishing his people by allowing a pagan nation to conquer them. But Habakkuk admitted growth in his spiritual perspective after he had listened to God declare his holiness and justice. 'You're in control, Lord. Even though the world is falling apart, I will still rejoice in you' (see *Hab 3*).

God may delay or say 'no' in order to engineer a total answer. For hundreds of years the Israelites prayed for their Messiah, but he came only when it was the 'fullness of time'.

Corrie ten Boom prayed that her sister would be healed at Ravensbruck, a concentration camp where they both were imprisoned. But her sister died. When Corrie was released she learned that her sister, had she lived, would have had to remain in the concentration camp without her. 'I have praised and thanked my Lord for that unanswered prayer,' she said. 'Just imagine how it would have been if she had been healed and would have had to stay in that hell of Ravensbruck without me. I would have returned to my homeland tormented by the consciousness of her suffering. I saw God's side of the embroidery.' God's 'no' to Corrie's prayer resulted in a worldwide ministry of grace and forgiveness.

God may delay his answer to teach us the wisdom of his silence. Sometimes we may not know the outcome of a prayer until we set foot in heaven. Then we'll know that it was answered, but not in ways we understood at the time.

Martin Luther said, 'I have held many things in my hands, and lost them all. But whatever I put in God's hands, that I still possess.' This is the picture of prevailing prayer. By putting our desires in his hands, we'll possess his blessings. And while the path up Prayer Mountain may be steep and tiring, it's often God's way of strengthening us to receive his answer.

SUNDAY 14 OCTOBER

A God of Unfailing Love

Psalm 21

'For the king trusts in the LORD; through the unfailing love of the Most High he will not be shaken' (v. 7, NIV).

Psalm 21 is a song of praise for victories granted to the king. The king over Israel was more than a military leader, he was also God's appointed representative, charged with directing the affairs of both state and religion. A return from battle or a coronation ceremony provided occasion for God's covenant with his people in the entire life of the nation to be remembered and reaffirmed. In this liturgy the king and the people recall that victory and deliverance have not been achieved, and will not be achieved, on the basis of military strength alone, but only in the strength of God.

Psalm 21 looks back to the past, stands in the present and faces the future. The remembrance of the past recalls the victories won as a result of God's activity (*vv. 2–6*). Because God has acted so decisively in the past, he can be counted upon in the future to grant victory again to his people (*vv. 8–12*). But it is the present moment, where past and future come together, that forms the central point of proclamation in this liturgy (*v. 7*).

As the king has trusted in the past, so his present and future security come from God's unfailing love. The Hebrew for the phrase 'unfailing love' denotes befriending. Appeal to God's unfailing love, kindness and mercy is frequent in the Old Testament, since it summarises all that God covenanted to show to Israel. This psalm is both praise and prayer – praise for what God has already done, and prayer that, as in the past, so in the future, he will continue to be a God of blessing.

Called upon one day to do a daunting task, I set out, feeling fearful of failure. On the way I stopped and read one of God's 'unfailing' promises: 'But I trust in your unfailing love' (*Psalm 13:5*). There in the centre of that word 'unfailing' lay my word 'fail', wrapped around with God's love.

Today, hunt out three promises of God's 'unfailing love' in the Psalms and rest your load on them.

MARK'S GOSPEL 4–7

Introduction

Mark's Gospel began with a sense of urgency and excitement. The first three chapters (see *WoL 25 June – 21 July 2001*) show Jesus in action at the beginning of his ministry. Wherever he goes, people are healed, forgiven and challenged. But while many turn to follow him, there are others who turn away.

The readings over the next three weeks cover Jesus' continued ministry in Galilee. His teaching in parables allows us to stop and listen carefully before we are plunged back into the account which is splashed with the colour of healings, a miraculous feeding, the calming of a storm and the expulsion of demons.

We also see Jesus sending out his disciples to multiply his ministry. They have had opportunity to observe his example. Now, having served their apprenticeship, it is time for them to go out in his name and with his authority to teach and heal. And so the news of the kingdom of God spreads but, as it does, the opposition heats up. John is beheaded in prison, Jesus' hometown crowd rejects him and the Pharisees come to check him out.

Over everything that happens hovers the question, 'Who is this man?' While demons seem to know the answer, those closest to Jesus still seem unable to understand just who he is.

As we read, may we be caught up in the movement and drama of these chapters. In the process, may we encounter the living Lord moving deeper into our lives, and moving us more effectively out into the world, to multiply his ministry in our day.

MONDAY 15 OCTOBER

A Lavish Sower

Mark 4:1–9

'He taught them many things by parables, and in his teaching said: "Listen!" ' (vv. 2,3, NIV).

The parable of the sower marks a new stage in Jesus' ministry. Earlier verses have referred to his teaching, but this is the first time that Mark gives us a parable about it. Jesus' question in 4:13 suggests that understanding this parable will help to unlock the meaning of all his teaching.

A parable is literally 'something thrown beside something else', or a comparison, an earthly story with a heavenly meaning. Jesus used this teaching method to make people listen. There was a familiarity, an everyday-ness, in his parables, whether they were about seeds, weeds or pearls. They may sound spontaneous, but Jesus was a skilled storyteller and his craft was revealed in the response of those who listened. Some heard and were amazed, while others were puzzled and infuriated. The key to hearing them was just that – hearing, not just superficially, but with what someone has called 'the third ear'. This parable begins and ends with a challenge to 'listen' (*v. 3*) and 'hear' (*v. 9*).

The sower sows liberally, scattering seed on a hardened pathway, a rocky terrain, among thorn bushes, as well as on ground that looks fertile. To modern church growth-attuned ears, such sowing sounds wasteful. The Pharisees would agree. They would certainly limit the terrain where the seed is sown. Lepers, sinners and tax-collectors would be classed as barren soil and not worth the waste of seed.

But the sower of Jesus' parable is not afraid to risk scattering his seeds wherever they may fall. In spite of hungry birds, shallow soil and an abundance of thorns, he will have a harvest from the ground. The sower is a picture of Jesus and the soils represent the degrees of receptivity in the hearts of people. The Pharisees themselves will be soil least receptive to the seed. But Jesus still sows lavishly. In spite of apparent failure, unbelief or opposition, he knows that a harvest will come. The word of God will not fail!

Prayer

Lord, let me hear, really hear, your word in my heart today.

TUESDAY 16 OCTOBER

Insiders and Outsiders

Mark 4:10–20

'He told them, "The secret of the kingdom of God has been given to you. But to those on the outside everything is said in parables" ' (v. 11, NIV).

Jesus speaks the parable of the sower from his boat pulpit to a crowd gathered on the shore. When he finishes, the disciples and some others press in to hear the meaning behind the story. To this close-gathered group of insiders, the mystery of the kingdom is revealed, while to those outside, everything comes in riddles. Jesus' teaching in parables separated those who were serious in seeking after God from those who were curious and just looking for a religious sideshow.

Being Jesus' disciples does not mean that they automatically understand all he says. They too need to press in, to ask questions, to listen carefully to his explanations. The difference between the insiders and 'those on the outside' is that they are not indifferent. The fact that Jesus explains the parable in private does not mean that this is a closed group with everyone else excluded. Others simply do not regard what he says to be critical enough to bother hearing his explanation.

But on many occasions Jesus will caution this insider group to pay heed to how they listen. A listening 'insider' response on one occasion will not mean that one is immune from the danger of becoming an 'outsider'. The pattern will be:

- Look. Do you understand? Look again.
- Listen. Do you understand? Listen again.

The religious authorities (*2:1–3:6*), his nearest relatives (*3:31–35*) and even his disciples (*8:14–21*) will so often look but see nothing special. They will listen, but fail to really hear. They are not lacking in intelligence, but they are hard of heart. If they fail to understand this parable, how will they understand the parable of the cross and resurrection? One will betray him, another deny him. They will all flee, leaving him to die alone. But others, like the Syrophoenician woman (*7:26*) and Blind Bartimaeus (*10:46*) will show the faith of 'insiders'.

Prayer

Lord, I want to be an 'insider' with a listening, open heart, fertile soil for your word to take root and grow.

WEDNESDAY 17 OCTOBER

Lamps and Listening

Mark 4:21–25

'Do you bring in a lamp to put it under a bowl or a bed? Instead, don't you put it on its stand?' (v. 21, NIV).

The illustrations of the lamp and the measure in these verses continue the tone of Jesus' explanation to his disciples and others around him when they come privately, asking him about the parable of the sower (*vv. 10–12*). We need to read these verses with our ears open and our senses attuned to what Jesus is saying, for his explanation still sounds mysterious.

A lamp, of course, is only effective when put on a stand so that its light can shine unhindered. This is the normal, expected function of a lamp. If it does not help people to see, it is useless. But the story of this lamp is placed in the context of other parables about the kingdom which speak of hiddenness. It is as if Jesus is saying, 'The lamp is here, and its light will one day shine clearly, but, for the moment, it has a secret, hidden presence. This is God's purpose.'

Jesus himself, by his own admission, came as 'the light of the world' (*John 8:12*). With his entry into human life, the light had indeed come, but it was not seen or recognised by many. He spoke in riddling parables, he commended strength by way of weakness, he predicted triumph through suffering. Even for those closest to him, the full significance of his life and ministry would only become clear after his death on the cross and his resurrection.

For those whose eyes were blinded and ears deafened by the dazzling sights and sounds of the world, Jesus knew that the kingdom would never really come. So he says again: 'Listen. Do you understand? Listen again.'

The parable of the measure refers to ways people respond to the light. Those who do not hear well will lose everything, as they rest content in their indifference. Those who do hear well will get more explanation and eventual understanding of God's purposes.

To reflect on

The one who rejects the truth has everything to lose; the one who risks faith in what now lies hidden has everything to gain.

THURSDAY 18 OCTOBER

A Growing Seed

Mark 4:26–29

'This is what the kingdom of God is like. A man scatters seed on the ground' (v. 26, NIV).

I am grateful to live in a country where fresh fruits and vegetables in season are abundantly available at the local supermarket. But I recall a far deeper gratitude at seeing plants sprout and grow in our garden in Zambia. With no well-stocked supermarket nearby, our physical well-being depended largely on what we could grow. With childlike wonder we would welcome the first signs of growth.

Mark writes again about seeds, emphasising in this parable the mysterious power of the seed itself. The farmer scatters his seed and then goes about his everyday routine. He sleeps, he rises, night and day. Meantime, the seed sprouts and grows. The seed holds within itself the secret of its growth, and the earth produces 'all by itself' (*v. 28*). Whatever happens under the ground eventually becomes visible. The farmer does not cause the growth; in fact he has no idea how it happens. The growth of the seed into a stalk, a head and then the full grain suggests an appointed order of development that can be neither hurried nor delayed. When the seed is fully grown, the farmer puts his sickle to the grain, for the harvest has come.

This parable needs to be understood in the light of the other parables that surround it. Like the seed, the kingdom of God is hidden, but it is silently and steadily working to produce the harvest that God intends. In this in-between time in which we live, we need to shake off discouragement and learn to look at the world as Jesus sees it, with seeds sown everywhere preparing for the harvest.

The parable assures us that when we sow God's seed, it will accomplish his purpose. In spite of the mysterious hiddenness of the kingdom, and in spite of setbacks, God's promise is that his word will not return empty, but will accomplish what he desires and achieve the purpose for which he sent it (see *Isa 55:11*).

Prayer

'I planted the seed . . . God . . . makes things grow' (1 Cor 3:6,7). Lord, help me to be faithful in doing my part.

FRIDAY 19 OCTOBER

From Small Beginnings

Mark 4:30–34

'The kingdom of God . . . is like a mustard seed, which is the smallest seed you plant in the ground' (vv. 30,31, NIV).

The smallest seed known to a Palestinian farmer or gardener was the mustard seed. It was cultivated for its leaves as well as its grains, being considered beneficial for health. A mustard seed was proverbially 'the smallest possible thing'. For instance, 'faith as small as a mustard seed' (*Matt 17:20*) was the least possible, the barest minimum. But scripted into the DNA structure of a microscopic mustard seed is a power to transform itself into something dramatically different.

Jesus again used a familiar, everyday object to make a startling comparison. 'You see what happens to a mustard seed when it is planted? It looks small and insignificant, but it will grow into a six- to ten-foot-high tree with big branches to give shade to the birds of the air.' The same thing, Jesus implied, is true of the kingdom of God. From small beginnings – an unknown rabbi with a ragtag bunch of followers – a mighty worldwide community of believers would grow. What God would accomplish through the life, death and resurrection of Jesus would indeed be extraordinary.

As Jesus spoke his parable, the kingdom of God was already present, but it was quiet and hidden from view. Religious leaders would misunderstand it. Jesus' own family would miss it. Even the disciples, his inner group of followers, at times would fail to recognise it. But it was already growing, evolving, making an impact upon the world that none of those who were at the beginning (*1:1*) would have guessed possible.

From those insignificant beginnings in Galilee, the Church has grown into something like a large tree, where people from all nations of the world can find shelter. 'There before me was a great multitude that no-one could count, from every nation, tribe, people and language' (*Rev 7:9*). A day will come when all the world will see the greatness and power of God's kingdom.

To reflect on

Look what God is doing! No matter how insignificant you or your part of the kingdom may seem, you are an indispensable part of God's great design.

SATURDAY 20 OCTOBER

Panic and Peace

Mark 4:35–41

'They were terrified and asked each other, "Who is this? Even the wind and the waves obey him!" ' (v. 41, NIV).

The Sea of Galilee, 680 feet below sea level and surrounded by hills, was notorious for its storms. They would strike suddenly, without warning, turning a fishing trip or a peaceful excursion into a nightmare.

It seems it was the end of a long, exhausting day of preaching and healing, when Jesus urged his disciples to set sail for the other side of the lake. Leaving the crowds, and people in other boats, Jesus lay down on a cushion in the stern and went to sleep. How human Jesus is! And how human the disciples! In spite of being seasoned fishermen, they were terrified by a sudden furious squall that threatened to swamp the boat.

Jesus' peaceful sleep in the midst of the raging storm was a sign of his trust in God. The disciples, however, interpreted his peaceful rest as indifference. 'Don't you care that we are about to perish?' they wailed as they shook him awake. Their tone contrasts sharply with the sad tone he uses later in Gethsemane when, needing the strength of their company, he found them heavy-eyed and sleeping (*14:40*).

The early symptoms of heavy eyes that cannot see appear in this scene, as their fear in the face of the storm threatens to overwhelm them. Jesus arises and speaks. He answers their anxious cries by rebuking the wind, using the same expression as when he told the demons to be quiet (*1:25*): 'Be muzzled!' With that command, the sea becomes calm. Wide-eyed and still terrified, the disciples turn from the water to the one who stands before them. Who is this man who has such godlike power over the elements?

The serenity of his sleep in the face of disaster, the authority with which he rebukes the chaotic powers of nature, and the reverential awe engendered in the disciples testify to them – and to us – that in this man the power and presence of God are mightily at work.

To reflect on

'Faith in God is less apt to proceed from miracles, than miracles from faith in God.'

Frederick Buechner

SUNDAY 21 OCTOBER

A Cry of Abandonment

Psalm 22

'My God, my God, why have you forsaken me?' (v. 1, NIV).

Lament, prayer and praise – these aspects of worship come together in Psalm 22. The psalmist is close to death, but the darkest part of his suffering is the sense of being abandoned by God. The history of his people, and his own life experience from the time of his birth, tell him that the covenant-making God can be depended upon to deliver his people. But his experience now tells him otherwise. His cry to God has been unceasing day and night, but is met with only silence. In stark contrast, the people around him are full of mocking, insulting words. They treat him like a worm, the lowest of the low, tainted with decay and death.

In desperation he moves from lament to prayer, begging God to be near. Enemies who are like strong bulls, roaring hungry lions, prowling dogs surround him. He is not yet dead but already they are dividing up his clothing. He is washed out and washed up. Again he begs God to be near and to deliver him.

Suddenly an answer comes. God has heard, deliverance is on its way. Suffering and scorn give way to sustenance, fear changes to fellowship, anguish to acceptance. Having begun his lament in utter desolation, he ends in a sweep of cosmic praise, calling his fellow worshippers to join in praise to God.

Behind this psalm stands the shadow of Calvary. Jesus so identified with the loneliness and suffering of the psalmist that he cried out these same words, 'My God, my God, why have you forsaken me?' as he hung on the cross (see *Matt 27:46; Mark 15:34*). In the suffering of Jesus we see God entering into the world of those who suffer and die. Because God in Jesus has experienced that desolation, he can offer comfort to those who walk now where the psalmist walked.

To reflect on

In Jesus' death and resurrection, this cry of abandonment has been answered for all time.

MONDAY 22 OCTOBER

A Wild Thing

Mark 5:1–13

'When Jesus got out of the boat, a man with an evil spirit came from the tombs to meet him' (v. 2, NIV).

Reaching land on the Gerasene side of the Sea of Galilee, Jesus steps out of the boat and into a confrontation with a demon-possessed man. Everything about this man is pitiful. He lives among tombs in the caves. Such places were known to be the haunt of demons, and considered dangerous and unclean. He may have survived by feeding off food that had been left for the dead. The tattered remnants of his clothing symbolise the wreckage of his life.

His wild behaviour terrifies the community in which he lived. They have tried to bind him, but he is powerful enough to snap the fetters and chains like string. His fierce strength cannot be subdued. He has been treated like a wild animal that cannot be tamed, and he acts like one, roaming free and uncontrollable. He has been banished from society and must dwell with those whose sleep will not be disturbed by his shrieks echoing through the night as he slashes his body with stones. He belongs to no one, a wild thing, lost and tormented.

The demons within cause him to rush at Jesus. These evil spirits recognise Jesus' divine origin and tremble in his presence. They know they have met their match, but they will not give up without a fight. Using the man as a mouthpiece, they shout, 'Jesus, Son of the Most High God' (*v.* 7) and try to persuade him to leave them alone.

Jesus counters by asking their name. The demons evade the question by answering with a number – 'Legion' – the 6,000 foot soldiers in a Roman regiment. Jesus, who has just demonstrated his dominion over the sea, does not need to know the names of the evil spirits in order to drive them out. Calmly he gives the word. In one action, unclean spirits and unclean animals are both wiped out, and a human being is cleansed and restored.

To reflect on

'Before my conversion I was a zoo of lusts, a bedlam of ambitions, a nursery of fears, a harem of fondled hatreds. My name was legion.'

C. S. Lewis

TUESDAY 23 OCTOBER

Pig Lovers, Unite!

Mark 5:14–20

'When they came to Jesus, they saw the man who had been possessed by the legion of demons, sitting there, dressed and in his right mind; and they were afraid' (v. 15, NIV).

First it was Miss Piggy, star of the *Muppet Show*, and then it was Babe. Such pigs, if it doesn't seem an insult to call them that, have 'humanised' the species, making them cute and adorable pets, if not full family members.

The pigs in this story were not family pets, but they were a means of livelihood, and their lemming-like destruction in the water causes a startling reaction in the townspeople. Having heard about the incident, many people come to see for themselves. Their reaction is one of fear, not at what has happened to their livelihood, but at what has happened to the tomb-dweller who is now sitting sanely and disciple-like at Jesus' feet. The community had desperately and unsuccessfully tried to tame him with chains and fetters. Jesus has freed him with a word.

Such power is hard to handle or even understand, and they beg Jesus to leave. They are more comfortable with the malevolent forces that take captive human beings and destroy minds than they are with the one who can expel them. They can cope with the odd demon-possessed wild man who terrorises the neighbourhood. But they want to keep someone with Jesus' power at a distance – preferably on the other side of the sea. They obviously consider him more dangerous than the demons. They are another example of outsiders who see but do not see, who hear but do not hear (*4:10–12*).

They beg him to go, and the recently restored man begs to go with him. Jesus refuses his request, sending him back home to be re-united with his family. Jesus also reverses his usual demand for silence by telling the man to spread the news of God's merciful dealings. The man is not simply to tell people about the miracle that has happened to him, but what that miracle signifies – God has been at work! Jesus may grant the community's wish for him to go, but he leaves behind the disturbing evidence of his presence.

To reflect on

Where Jesus is, God is at work!

WEDNESDAY 24 OCTOBER

A Desperate Father

Mark 5:21–24

'One of the synagogue rulers, named Jairus, came there. Seeing Jesus, he fell at his feet' (v. 22, NIV).

The fifth chapter of Mark's Gospel contains three powerful word pictures of desperate people – a demon-possessed man, a father whose daughter lies at death's door, and a woman who touches Jesus' garment in hope of a miracle. The stories have parallels of fear and faith, desperation and deliverance, and they merge together to paint a picture of Jesus who is equal to any threat that may shatter human life. Much of the power of these stories lies in their contrasts.

Jesus comes from restoring a raving, tormented wild man near the caves of Gerasa. Returning to the other side of the lake, he is waylaid again, this time by a ruler of the local synagogue. The ruler was the administrative head, responsible for the allocation and carrying out of duties. As such, he would be an important and highly respected man in the community. This man is well-bred, well-groomed and well-heeled.

In his time of fear and desperation, however, personal pride and dignity, and maybe even prejudice against Jesus, are laid aside as he falls at Jesus' feet and begs him to come to his home to bring healing to his daughter. Although he is a man of means, having a large household, he takes the same pose as the leper who came, empty-handed and desperate, kneeling before Jesus and begging for his healing (*1:40*). His rank as a leader in an institution that has become hostile to Jesus does not disqualify him from Jesus' attention.

Jesus moves to go with him, but an anonymous woman interrupts the rush to the dying girl. Jairus is left to wait. What might he be thinking as he chafes at the delay? 'Why is he not coming? I was first in line. He should take care of my problem before hers.' This very delay, although painful for the distraught father, adds tension to the story, and fibre to his faith.

To reflect on

Waiting for God's answer gives us a choice – frustration or faith. Which one do you choose today?

THURSDAY 25 OCTOBER

A Grey Woman

Mark 5:25–34

'A woman was there who had been subject to bleeding for twelve years' (v. 25, NIV).

If I were an artist, I would need a large amount of grey to paint this woman. Everything about her is washed-out and colourless. She is anonymous, a non-person. Her abnormal, perpetual bleeding for twelve years has made her ritually unclean (see *Lev 15:25–27*), which means her impurity is transferable. Thus she is rejected and excluded from normal social contact and from places of worship. She suffers physically every day with the signs of mortality. Her complaint makes marriage and childbearing impossible. What's more, she has become impoverished after wasting her living on doctors who have been unable to cure her.

Within this grey figure, however, there is a glimmer of faith. With an 'If only' on her heart, she edges her way through the crowd, eyes downcast, head covered. She creeps up behind Jesus and touches the edge of his cloak. Immediately her flow of blood stops. Also immediately, Jesus knows that power has gone forth from him. He puzzles the disciples by asking who in the throng has touched him. 'How should we know?' they respond. 'Everybody is touching you.'

But only one was healed, and she is seized with fear. The fear may have been guilt that she has stolen power from him and somehow passed her impurity on to him. She may have expected a scolding rather than a blessing. Her fear may, like that of the disciples on the lake (*4:40*), come from a terrifying question that forms in her mind, 'Who is this, who can heal me without even a word, when countless others could not?'

In identifying her, Jesus forces her to acknowledge publicly that he is the source of her healing. As she falls at his feet, he blesses her and announces that her faith has made her well. He tells her to go in peace – *shalom* – wholeness, well-being, prosperity, security, friendship and salvation. She heads for home, her body whole, her eyes dancing, her cheeks flushed pink.

To reflect on

Into which area of your life would God speak* shalom *to you today?

FRIDAY 26 OCTOBER

Faith in Face of Hopelessness

Mark 5:35–43

'Ignoring what they said, Jesus told the synagogue ruler, "Don't be afraid; just believe" ' (v. 36, NIV).

The spotlight returns to Jairus as he waits, worried to death by his own desperate situation, while Jesus attends to someone else's need. His balance of fear and faith is threatened with the arrival of the bad news that his daughter has died. 'Why bother the teacher any more?' he is asked, but Jesus answers for him, 'Don't be afraid, just keep on believing.' He had shown faith in coming to Jesus in the first place; now he must continue, even in the face of hopelessness.

He leads Jesus to his house and there they discover the grievous chorus of those who have already gathered to mourn the girl's death. Jesus' announcement, without even seeing her, that she is not dead but sleeping, is met with jeering laughter. Of course she is dead. Jesus, however, can turn a raging storm into a great calm, a wild thing into a normal man, and the laughter of scorn into the laughter of joy. The scepticism of the crowd puts them outside, beyond the reach of the miracle that is about to happen.

In private, with only the parents and his closest friends, Jesus grasps the little girl's hand to raise her up, saying, *'Talitha koum.'* This is no magical incantation, but an ordinary command, simply spoken. He tells the relieved mother to give her something to eat, and tells them all to keep the matter quiet.

The time is not right for word to be spread of Jesus' power to raise the dead. Until he himself is resurrected, death can only be kept at bay. Then it will be conquered forever (*1 Cor 15:54–57*). Jesus also knows the crowd well enough to realise that a miracle-worker, a magician healer who can do wonders, will attract a following, but for all the wrong reasons. His healing of this girl must be seen, as with all he does, as evidence of the presence of the kingdom of God.

To reflect on

Notice how, in this story, faith leads to healing, not the other way round.

SATURDAY 27 OCTOBER

A Prophet Without Honour

Mark 6:1–6a

'When the Sabbath came, he began to teach in the synagogue, and many who heard him were amazed. "Where did this man get these things?" ' (v. 2, NIV).

Jesus moves from the area where his ministry has had life-changing impact, and returns to his own home town of Nazareth. Again he teaches in the synagogue on the Sabbath, and as before, 'many who heard him were amazed' (see *1:22*).

This time, however, it was not amazement at the authority with which he spoke, but rather a kind of suspicion. Having heard his wisdom and seen his miracles, they ask, 'Where did this man get these things?' The people around him believe they know all about him and his family background. They know his mother and his brothers and sisters. 'Isn't he the carpenter?' they ask, meaning, 'Isn't he a common labourer like the rest of us?' 'How can someone so ordinary do marvels and speak wisdom?' 'How can this one who is so familiar to us be God's anointed?' They are suspicious and annoyed. Who does he think he is? This is the scandal of the gospel. A local yokel the Son of God? Hardly!

Jesus responds to their scepticism by stating that a prophet is without honour among his own people. This provides an explanation for their unbelief, but not an excuse. In referring to himself as a prophet, Jesus evokes a powerful scriptural image. He has come like a prophet and like a prophet he will be rejected. The martyrdom of the prophet John will soon be described (*6:17–29*). Jesus' rejection in his own home town is merely the beginning of rejection by his own people whom he came to deliver, a rejection that will culminate in Jerusalem.

Finally, he can do no miracles in Nazareth except heal a few people. As they were amazed at hearing him (*v. 2*), so he is amazed at their lack of faith (*v. 6*). He moves away from the synagogue, back to the villages where people can come to him openly.

To reflect on

First they asked 'What?' (1:27). Then they asked 'Who?' (4:41). Now they ask 'Where?' (6:2). Which question is a stumbling block to your faith?

SUNDAY 28 OCTOBER

The Shepherd Psalm

Psalm 23

'The LORD is my shepherd, I shall not be in want' (v. 1, NIV).

This psalm must be the most beloved of all the psalms. I learned it as a child, the simple and beautiful poetry of the King James version making the learning unforgettable. The beauty of the psalm lies also in its expression of serene confidence found in a trusting relationship with God.

Whatever our human situation, we need to know that we are not alone in the world. The name given to Jesus at his birth was 'Immanuel' – 'God with us' (*Matt 1:23*). At the end of his earthly life, he promised his disciples, 'Surely I am with you' (*Matt 28:20*). Like a child who clutches the hand of a loving parent as they walk together past a ferocious dog or down a dark alleyway, we need to know that the hand of God is constantly holding ours. The psalmist had learned:

- The Lord is a personal shepherd (*v. 1*). He wrote from the heart of a faith community, but he writes of 'my shepherd', claiming a personal association with God.
- The Lord is a present shepherd (*v. 4*). Even when facing a great danger or surrounded by enemies, the psalmist knew that God was with him.
- The Lord is a protecting shepherd (*v. 4*). The Palestinian shepherd normally carried two implements, a club (or rod) to fight off wild beasts, and a crook (or staff) to guide and control the sheep. So the Lord both protects his flock and guides them forward to fresh pasture. When the psalmist's way went through the valley of the shadow of death itself, even there God continued to be his protecting shepherd.
- The Lord is a providing shepherd (*v. 5*). Just as God provided for his people after their exodus from Egypt (see *Deut 2:7*), so he leads his people to lush pastures and refreshing water, and to a banqueting table.

May you know the Lord as your shepherd today.

To reflect on

The movement of this psalm can be summed up by joining the first, the middle and the last words: 'The Lord . . . with me . . . for ever.'

MONDAY 29 OCTOBER

Men on a Mission

Mark 6:6b–13

'Calling the Twelve to him, he sent them out two by two and gave them authority over evil spirits' (v. 7, NIV).

Jesus began his public ministry by calling Israel to repentance (*1:14–15*). Now he expands that mission by sending out the Twelve to preach repentance, to cast out demons, and to anoint the sick. He gives them authority over unclean spirits (see *3:15*) and sends them out two by two. Such teamwork would not only provide a measure of protection, but would also satisfy the requirement of two or three witnesses (see *Deut 17:6*).

With their marching orders comes no leadership manual on how to raise the dead or exorcise demons – rather, a detailed list of instructions on what not to pack for the journey. He allows them to take a staff and to wear sandals, but they are to take no provisions, no beggar's bag, no money and no change of clothing. The list reflects the character of their mission. They are not to travel first-class, nor stay at the best hotels. They are to go humbly, depending on God to provide food and lodgings in the villages they enter. They are to go as the poor to those who are also poor and hungry.

This send-off parallels the one given to the children of Israel as they set out into the desert, 'with your cloak tucked into your belt, your sandals on your feet and your staff in your hand' (*Exod 12:11*). Just as God sustained Israel in the desert, so he will provide now for the disciples. Jesus expects they will encounter rejection, and so he prepares them. If a place neither receives nor hears them, they are to shake the dust from their feet and leave. There is no time to waste arguing.

The time for watching Jesus 'do ministry' is over. Practice in the task of mission will come, no longer in the classroom of their close relationship with him, but out there, in the world where rejection stalks, where demons shriek and where people's needs are overwhelming.

To reflect on

With what feelings did they go? Trepidation and trust? Is it so different for you and me today?

TUESDAY 30 OCTOBER

The Tragic Consequences of a Troubled Conscience

Mark 6:14–29

'King Herod heard about this, for Jesus' name had become well known. Some were saying, "John the Baptist has been raised from the dead, and that is why miraculous powers are at work in him" ' (v. 14, NIV).

Herod Antipas, who ruled over Galilee and Perea, was officially a tetrarch (ruler over a fourth part of a region), but his popular title was 'King Herod'. Hearing the reports of Jesus' growing reputation, Herod is gripped with fear. The same questions that puzzled Jesus' home town now hover over Herod – 'Who is this man, and where does he get his power?' Herod comes to the frightening conclusion that John has been resurrected and has come back to haunt him. That's a fearsome prospect for the man who had ordered John's death!

John had publicly reproached Herod for marrying Herodias, who was already the wife of his half-brother. Herodias nursed a grudge against John and looked for an opportunity to silence him, but Herod seemed to have an awed fascination with the man and liked to listen to him.

Opportunity came for Herodias at a birthday banquet when her daughter danced before Herod and his guests. Flushed with drink, he offered the girl whatever she wanted, even half of his kingdom. It was not his to give away, of course, but Herodias saw her opportunity and told the girl to ask for the head of John the Baptist. Suddenly sober and distressed, Herod was forced to choose between his honour in keeping the rash promise made in front of his guests, and the life of an innocent man whom he had both feared and liked. So John died, because of the intrigue of an offended woman and the weakness of her drunken husband.

This account, sandwiched between the sending out of the Twelve (*v. 7*) and their return (*v. 30*), casts a shadow of death and danger over the disciples' mission. They too will be handed over and will have to stand before kings (*13:9*). The power to do miracles will not exempt them from suffering and death. The world is full of evil people who will try to silence the messengers of God and their disturbing message. But they will not succeed.

To reflect on

The kingdom of God advances, in spite of every worldly power that challenges it.

WEDNESDAY 31 OCTOBER

Compassion Fatigue

Mark 6:30–44

'Because so many people were coming and going that they did not even have a chance to eat, he said to them, "Come with me by yourselves to a quiet place and get some rest" ' (v. 31, NIV).

The apostles ('sent ones') return to Jesus and give a report of their preaching mission. They hear the tragic news of John the Baptist's death. The crowds continue to come in droves. There is no time to eat. Mark reports these incidents factually, but leaves us to imagine the feelings of the disciples at this time. It's not hard to imagine these disciples suffering from overwhelming exhaustion, or what is referred to nowadays as 'compassion fatigue'. Jesus recognises the cost of their giving out, and leads them to a solitary place where they can get some rest. Their relief, however, is short-lived. The crowds also seem to know about this solitary place and they race there ahead of the little group in the boat.

While the disciples may be muttering 'Oh no!' in irritation, Jesus has an altogether different reaction. He sees the crowd as sheep without a shepherd, and his first response is to teach them. The disciples' own needs are once more put on hold. Late in the day they urge Jesus to send the people away to buy some food. To their shock, he orders them to feed the crowd. 'Excuse me, Jesus, don't you recall telling us not so long ago not to take any bread or money with us?'

Their alarm makes the miracle even more potent. Empty-handed, they have nothing left to give. Famished, they are aware of their own hunger and weariness. Drained of energy and faith, they still have no understanding that Jesus has divine resources when their own fail. Between them they rustle up five loaves and two fish. In a gesture which foreshadows the Last Supper (*14:22*), Jesus gives thanks, breaks the meagre meal, then hands it back to the disciples for distribution.

I gave my lunch to Jesus and let him do the rest,
He took the humble bread I had, gave thanks and broke and blessed,
It fed a mighty multitude, my lunch that was so small,
In Jesus' hands it was enough to satisfy them all.

THURSDAY 1 NOVEMBER

An Evening Epiphany

Mark 6:45–52

'Immediately he spoke to them and said, "Take courage! It is I. Don't be afraid" ' (v. 50, NIV).

With the memory of the miraculous feeding still dancing in their minds, the disciples head across the lake to Bethsaida. Jesus, left alone, dismisses the satisfied crowd and seeks out his own solitary place to pray.

In the darkest hour of the night, however, and at the deepest part of the lake, the disciples are rowing strenuously but getting nowhere against the wind. Jesus sees their struggle and, during the early hours of the morning, walks across to them on the water. The phrase, 'he was about to pass by them' (*v. 48*), seems a strange comment. Was he being playful and wanting to surprise them by reaching the other side first? Was he testing their faith?

The word translated 'to pass by' suggests nothing playful or capricious on Jesus' part, but rather a desire to communicate something important about his identity by means of an unusual appearance. This is called an 'epiphany'. In the Old Testament Moses asked God to show him his glory and God responded by passing before him: 'When my glory passes by, I will put you in a cleft in the rock and cover you with my hand until I have passed by. Then I will remove my hand and you will see my back; but my face must not be seen' (*Exod 33:22–23*).

God could not be fully seen, but Jesus is fully recognisable. His greeting to the disciples on the water is not simply a cheery hello to calm their fears. He greets them with the words of divine revelation, 'I AM' (see *Exod 3:14*). Their terror at seeing what they think is a ghost is scarcely lessened as he climbs into the boat with them and the wind and waves die down.

To reflect on

I would not have called it an epiphany, but I recall a time I was turned down for something I really wanted. Distressed, I was planning to appeal against the decision, when Jesus spoke these same words to me, 'Don't be afraid. It is I.' Subsequent events proved that God was indeed in the decision.

FRIDAY 2 NOVEMBER

A Needy Crowd

Mark 6:53–56

'And wherever he went – into villages, towns or countryside – they placed the sick in the market-places. They begged him to let them touch even the edge of his cloak, and all who touched him were healed' (v. 56, NIV).

The boat lands, not at Bethsaida, but at Gennesaret, located on the west side of the Sea of Galilee. Once again the crowds press in with urgency. Mark uses just a few words to paint a scene of intense activity and clamour around Jesus.

The disciples may still be reeling from the terrifying appearance of the ghostlike Jesus out on the water. They may still be trying to understand what the feeding miracle was all about (see *v. 52*). The question 'Who is this man?' seems to hang more heavily than ever over the group, with none of them being any closer to really understanding. These disciples have had the privilege of being with Jesus since the beginning of his public ministry, seeing him deal with people, listening to him teach, but with every miraculous event they seem further away.

In contrast, the people of the Gennesaret region recognise Jesus and hurry to bring their sick people to him. These Gennesaret people were not 'insiders' as the disciples were (see *4:10*). They had not had the privilege of being with Jesus day after day, but they knew of his reputation as a healing man, and that was enough. So they bring their sick to the central market place and there Jesus heals them.

Even a touch of one of the tassels sewn on the lower corner of his cloak was enough for his healing power to be released. Unlike the woman with the bleeding who came furtively to touch his cloak (see *5:27*), these people come boldly and he does not stop them. He does not deny them their healing just because they do not understand, nor rebuke them for coming to get something from him, rather than to give him their allegiance.

The disciples do not know who he is, but the people of Gennesaret are convinced that he has power to heal, so they do not even stop to ask the question. Their great faith in Jesus' power contrasts with the little faith of the disciples.

To reflect on

Do you have the faith of an 'insider'?

SATURDAY 3 NOVEMBER

Clean Hands and a Pure Heart

Mark 7:1–23

'Listen to me, everyone, and understand this. Nothing outside a man can make him "unclean" by going into him. Rather, it is what comes out of a man that makes him "unclean" ' (vv. 14,15, NIV).

The group that now gathers around Jesus are not seekers wanting the 'inside' story on his teaching (see *4:10*), but religious leaders who have come once more from Jerusalem to check up on him. One thing they notice immediately is that Jesus' disciples eat with 'unclean', that is unwashed, hands. For the Pharisees, hand-washing was not a matter of hygiene, but purity. Jews became ceremonially defiled during the everyday circumstances of life, merely by contact with people, vessels or clothing. Such impurity had to be removed by a careful hand-washing ritual.

Instead of responding to the matter of defiled hands, Jesus raises the issue of what really defiles a person. He challenges the Pharisees' rigid and superficial religiosity, which gives attention to clean hands and looking good on the outside, but pays no attention to the morality that comes from a pure heart. He rebukes the way they use God as an excuse to avoid helping their families. The commandment for children to honour their parents (*Exod 20:12*) meant not just showing them respect, but also providing for their physical needs. The Pharisees would allow a son to get round that requirement by informing his parents that whatever financial support they might expect from him is 'Corban', that is dedicated to God, and therefore cannot be used to help them.

Jesus exposes the Pharisees' ways of setting their own traditions above God's will (*vv. 8,13*). They are concerned with surface impurity and piety, but he is concerned with internal impurity that cannot be washed away with water. Jesus' fiery response puzzles the disciples and privately they ask for an explanation. Dismayed at their lack of understanding, Jesus patiently explains that food cannot defile anyone. The only defilement they need worry about has to do with the heart, which is the centre of motivation and intention. The 'evil thoughts' and impure actions that proceed from that centre need more than a little water for cleansing!

To reflect on

'If your heart's all right, you'll do, you'll do! If your heart's all right, you'll do!'

John Gowans

SUNDAY 4 NOVEMBER

A Song to the King of Glory

Psalm 24

'Lift up your heads, O you gates; be lifted up, you ancient doors, that the King of glory may come in' (v. 7, NIV).

Slowly the colourful procession makes its way up the hill towards the temple. At the head of the group is the king with his attendants. Behind him comes the choir with the priests. At the back come worshippers – men, women and children. This procession is in commemoration of the Lord's entrance into Jerusalem, when David brought the ark from the house of Obed-edom to the city, following war against the Philistines. The Lord Almighty has triumphed over all his enemies and now comes in victory to his own city.

'Who may ascend the hill?' chant the pilgrims as they climb. The response is given, 'He who has clean hands and a pure heart', that is, guiltless actions and right attitudes. 'He will receive blessing from the LORD.' In blessing they continue their climb but arrive at the temple to find the doors closed. Those at the head of the procession call out for the doors to be opened, so that the King of glory may come in. The keepers of the gates call out their question, 'Who is this King of glory?' Outside, the pilgrims respond in unison, 'The LORD mighty in battle.' The exchange is repeated, the temple gates swing open and the people joyfully surge forward into the temple. Like the great doors, God's arms have been opened in welcome and blessing to his people.

Jesus called himself a gate for the sheep. Like the great doors of the temple, he is our entrance-way into the presence of God. We may not chant the pilgrim's question as we come to Sunday worship today but we need to ask it in our hearts, 'Am I worthy to come into God's presence?' Left to ourselves, the answer is, 'Of course not!' But by his death Jesus has opened up the way for us, and so we can come with the same pilgrim rejoicing.

You are the King of Glory.
You are the Prince of Peace.
You are the Lord of heav'n and earth.
You're the Son of righteousness.

Mavis Ford[5]

THE BOOK OF JOB

Introduction

Two separate incidents propelled me into this series on the book of Job. The first was being with a group of people one Saturday for a poetry workshop. As people introduced themselves, I was amazed at the number who spoke of a recent and still fresh experience of grief. The other incident was a TV documentary called *Tough Choices* which featured several couples who had to decide whether to continue with a pregnancy, given the high likelihood of a congenital deformity in the baby.

The question 'Why?' hangs heavily in the air for many people. Why does a spouse die suddenly? Why do accidents happen? Why does a child get leukaemia? Why is a baby born with a deformity? Why do bad things happen to good people?

The book of Job gives no easy answers to the question, 'Why?' What it does is take us on a journey through a good man's life as he is tested to the limits of his endurance, preached at by his friends and chastened by God. Job's 'why' questions finally find a place of rest as God lifts Job's eyes from his dust heap to a new perspective on his world.

His so-called friends saw Job's suffering as punishment for his sins. Job himself saw it as a moral outrage, given his life of integrity. The accuser saw it as the means of stripping Job of everything and turning him against God in anger and cursing. But God allowed suffering to test Job and eventually to bring him forth like gold that is tested and refined in fire.

Job's story is in many ways our own story, his journey through suffering a familiar landscape. It seemed appropriate to locate this series in November, just a few weeks before Christmas and all the colour and joy of the Advent season. To know that God is with us, 'Immanuel', especially in the midst of inexplicable suffering, is good news indeed.

MONDAY 5 NOVEMBER

Man of Blessing

Job 1:1–5

'In the land of Uz there lived a man whose name was Job. This man was blameless and upright; he feared God and shunned evil' (v. 1, NIV).

The opening verse of the book of Job introduces Job, the man of God, and gives us three details about him – his name, his location and his character. The land of Uz was not Israelite territory. The name 'Job' would have a foreign ring to it. These features give Job a sense of distance, making him like a mythical character in a 'once-upon-a-time' story. Job himself was a man of blameless and upright character who feared God and shunned evil. He was a man of integrity, a quality recognised by both God and Job's wife (see *2:3,9*).

He was a man of great wealth. The numbers used are symbolic of completeness and perfection. He had seven sons and three daughters, a total of ten children. Likewise, 7,000 sheep and 3,000 camels, a total of 10,000. He had a balanced distribution of 500 oxen and 500 donkeys. The word in Hebrew used for donkeys refers to females, which would be very valuable. Just as Job's piety is complete and perfect, so also are his family and property. It is not hard to believe that he is indeed the greatest person in his part of the world.

Although the word 'blessing' is not used, the description of this great and wealthy man suggests that he is indeed a righteous person blessed by God (see *Ps 112:1–3*).

As the spotlight moves onto Job's children, we get a further picture of untroubled bliss and harmony. Job's sons live like a king's sons, each in his own home, taking their turns (perhaps on birthday occasions) to host a family banquet to which their sisters are invited. At the end of each feast, Job, as father of the household, acts as priest on behalf of his family. Fearful that they may have sinned unknowingly, he offers sacrifice on their behalf. It is ironical that it is precisely Job's righteousness that will set in motion the events leading to the deaths of these children.

To reflect on

Was Job righteous because God blessed him, or did God bless him because Job was righteous?

TUESDAY 6 NOVEMBER

The Curtain is Drawn Back

Job 1:6–12

'One day the angels came to present themselves before the LORD, and Satan also came with them' (v. 6, NIV).

The first scene of Job's life is a picture of blessing. His righteousness and integrity, wealth and family happiness are all painted with bold brush strokes. In the second scene, however, a curtain is drawn back, revealing a dark shadow over the picture.

A heavenly court is taking place. Angels and other divine beings, including Satan, stand before God the King, receiving orders and reporting back from their missions. In response to God's question, Satan declares that he has been patrolling the earth. Before he can give his report, God throws the spotlight onto Job and challenges the accuser with a question. 'Have you considered my servant Job?' he asks. Job is not merely 'the greatest man among all the people of the East' (*1:3*); in God's eyes, 'there is no one on earth like him' (*v. 8*). God suggests that Job's perfect character gives the accuser no grounds for accusation.

Satan avoids the question and turns to Job's motivation for righteousness. 'You've put a hedge around him,' he says, 'and his household and livestock. He's pious because it's to his advantage to be so. But remove the hedge of protection, and you'll see piety turn to cursing.' God consents to the test, but insists that Job himself is unharmed. The scene ends dramatically. The accuser, having received a new commission, goes out from God's presence.

Edith Schaeffer[6] suggests that every Christian lives under the spotlight of God's blessing and Satan's accusation, just as Job did. The accuser looks at you and declares, 'Remove your hedge of blessing from that person, God. Inflict them with a sudden illness, a grievous loss, an impossible task or whatever, and you'll see their trust turn to cursing.' But God looks at you and responds, 'No, Satan, you're wrong. Look at my servant __________ (*insert your name here*). See how he or she trusts me, even in the midst of that illness, that loss, that overwhelming thing.'

To reflect on

Keep reading! The accuser will not have the last word in Job's life, or in yours!

WEDNESDAY 7 NOVEMBER

The First Test

Job 1:13–22

'Naked I came from my mother's womb, and naked I shall depart. The LORD gave and the LORD has taken away; may the name of the LORD be praised' (v. 21, NIV).

This scene opens on a family celebration and closes on a father stricken with grief. Four messengers come to Job, each with a report of terrible loss. His oxen and donkeys have been carried off by the Sabeans. Lightning has killed his vast flocks of sheep. Chaldean raiding parties have carried off his camels. Some servants have also died in each raid, until there are none left. Finally, his children have been killed when a tornado struck the house where they were banqueting. The completeness of Job's piety (*v. 1*) and the completeness of his blessing (*vv. 2–3*) are now matched by the completeness of his destruction (*vv. 14–19*).

These grievous messages are brought to Job in quick succession. There is no time for him to react to each individual loss. For a moment everything stands still as we wait for Job's response. At first he says nothing, but expresses himself in the ancient gestures of mourning. He tears his robe in grief and shaves his head. He falls to the ground, not in weeping, but in worship. When he does speak it is not the traditional language of funeral song or lament that he uses, but proverbial words from the wisdom tradition (see *Eccl 5:15*).

As he came forth, a naked body from his mother's womb, so he will depart, a naked body, taking nothing with him to the grave. The fragility of the gift of life and the desolation of the loss of life are endurable only if it is God who gives and God who takes away (see *Ps 104:27–30*). Job's words of blessing addressed to God are an act of worship that reaffirms their relationship. Not in spite of his loss, but precisely because of its overwhelming size, Job moves from the ritual of grief to words of blessing. We stand on holy ground as we watch and listen to this man.

To reflect on

Satan's prediction is proved wrong. 'In all this, Job did not sin by charging God with wrongdoing' (v. 22).

THURSDAY 8 NOVEMBER

The Second Test

Job 2:1–10

' "Skin for skin!" Satan replied. "A man will give all he has for his own life. But stretch out your hand and strike his flesh and bones, and he will surely curse you to your face" ' (v. 4, NIV).

The curtain is pulled back a little and we hear the heavenly dialogue take place once again. The conversation between God and the accuser is identical with the previous one (*1:7–8*), but new words break the repetition at verse 3b. God speaks of his servant Job as a man who holds on to his integrity even though Satan has persuaded God to remove the hedge of protection from around him.

Unwilling to concede defeat, the accuser quotes a saying that comes from the market place and has to do with comparative values. A person trying to trade for a skin would be willing to offer anything of value, up to an equivalent skin. So he argues, 'All that a man has he will give, up to his life' (*v. 4*). In other words, says the accuser, test this man's piety once and for all by removing the final prosperity he has, namely his own life. Let him be smitten so severely that he despairs of life and longs for death, and then you will hear him curse you. God once again places Job under the power of the accuser, this time preserving only his life.

The accuser departs from the presence of God, and immediately we see Job sitting among the ashes, the place of mourning, covered in skin sores from top to toe. In a culture where skin diseases evoked social revulsion and were often seen as a mark of divine displeasure, Job may have felt that the God he refused to curse had in fact cursed him. He engages in no new acts of mourning. His only response to this new, terrible suffering is a purely physical one. He picks up a piece of broken pot and scratches himself with it.

Job's wife breaks the silence. This woman has also lost everything, her income, her position, her ten children. In her mind, the options are clear – Job should curse God, and put himself out of his misery. For Job, it is not so simple.

To reflect on

What would you do?

FRIDAY 9 NOVEMBER

A Comforting Presence

Job 2:11–13

'They sat on the ground with him for seven days and seven nights. No-one said a word to him, because they saw how great his suffering was' (v. 13, NIV).

Hearing about Job's tragic losses, his three friends, Eliphaz, Bildad and Zophar, come to console him. Even at a distance, the sight of Job, changed almost beyond recognition, is enough to trigger off a deep wail of anguish. Weeping aloud and tearing their robes, they give full vent to their distress. As their wailing subsides, they sit down on the ground alongside Job. For seven days and seven nights no one speaks a word. Three friends and seven days – the numbers echo the perfection and completeness of Job's possessions in chapter 1. Now it is his suffering that is complete.

These three friends, traditionally called 'Job's comforters', are criticised for what they eventually do say to Job. Although they are known to be wise men, their wisdom will prove to be narrow-minded and unhelpful. But for the moment, in this scene of the story at least, they do two things well.

First, they come. They could no doubt have found excuses not to come. 'We wouldn't know what to say.' 'Perhaps he would prefer to be left on his own.' 'He might not want us to see him like this.' In spite of such doubts, they came 'to sympathise with him and to comfort him' (*v. 11*). Their very coming would be an expression of solidarity for Job in his grief.

Second, they sit with Job in silence for as long as he needs to do so. According to Jewish tradition, those who come to comfort someone in grief should not speak until the mourner speaks. Job's friends recognise that his grief is too deep to be healed with mere words, so they say nothing. Their compassionate (literally 'suffering with') presence and their respectful silence are the two great gifts they give to Job.

To reflect on

I have a friend whose husband died suddenly, leaving her devastated. For about a year afterwards, her corps officer went regularly every week to see her. 'Often we talked,' she told me, 'but many times we just sat in silence. Her presence was the greatest gift she could have given me.'

SATURDAY 10 NOVEMBER

Why?

Job 3:1–26

'Why is life given to a man whose way is hidden, whom God has hedged in?' (v. 23, NIV).

In February 1947 a plane bound for Ecuador crashed into a mountain. A young man from New York, Glenn Chambers, was one of the victims. He was on his way to begin a lifelong dream of a ministry with the radio station 'Voice of the Andes' when the tragedy happened. Before leaving Miami airport earlier that day, Glenn Chambers had dashed off a note to his mother using a piece of paper he picked up off the terminal floor. The scrap of paper was part of an advertisement and the word 'Why' was sprawled right across it. But between the writing and the delivery of that note, Glenn Chambers was killed. When his mother opened the note, the haunting question 'Why?' was staring up at her.[7]

It is the most searching, the most tormenting of questions. The young couple who long to have a baby but cannot; the parent who receives the deathly diagnosis; the wife who learns of her husband's tragic death; the father of five who loses his job; the young woman whose close friend commits suicide – they all cry out the question *'Why?'*

After seven days and seven nights of silence, Job's suffering finds its voice. Using the language of pain and lament, he curses the day he was born and cries out the bitter question, 'Why?' Why did God bring him to birth? Why was he not allowed to die on that first day? Why has the hedge of God's protection and blessing (see *1:10*) now become a hedge of turmoil and suffering, hemming him in and giving him no way out? Job is as close as he will ever come to cursing God, but he does not.

From all that he knows of God, Job holds on to three facts for dear life. They are simply:

- God is too kind to do anything cruel,
- too wise to make a mistake, and
- too deep to explain himself.

SUNDAY 11 NOVEMBER

Humility and Holiness

Psalm 25

'The LORD confides in those who fear him; he makes his covenant known to them' (v. 14, NIV).

The psalms progress from glad duty in Psalm 1 to utter delight in Psalm 150. But the journey through this songbook of the Bible plunges the worshipper into a world of enemies, personal restlessness and anguished lament. Psalm 25 is one of these 'honest-to-God' cries along the road.

Psalm 1 outlined the two ways that can be chosen in life – the way of the righteous and that of the wicked. Psalm 25 is the prayer of a person who has chosen to walk the righteous way, but is finding the way difficult. It is lined with enemies, waiting to get him, wanting to put him to shame by proving the powerlessness of his God. As well as these mocking spectators, he is plagued with internal taunts as he remembers the sins of his younger years and his wanderings from the path. Troubled from without and within, he stops for a moment on the way. He knows he cannot turn back, but scarcely knows how to continue. And so he prays that God will show him the way and help him to keep walking.

'Remember your faithful, promised love to me,' he cries, 'but don't remember my sins and rebellion against you.' In humility (*humus* = 'earth'), the psalmist acknowledges his own earthiness and his need of God's forgiveness. The psalmist paints a picture of the person who lives under God's blessing and favour. Fear is the starting point for this relationship. Not a cowering fear but a reverential awe, linked with a deep love for God. God will treat such a person as his friend, confiding in him, just as close friends tell each other their secrets.

Longing for such an intimate relationship and for the clear direction it will bring to his life, the psalmist prays for God's protection. He asks for integrity and uprightness to be his bodyguards. Uprightness will say, 'This is God's way for me', and integrity will say, 'I will walk consistently in it.'

To reflect on

Humility – recognising my earthiness; Holiness – recognising his purity.

MONDAY 12 NOVEMBER

Eliphaz's Assumption

Job 4:17–5:18

'Blessed is the man whom God corrects; so do not despise the discipline of the Almighty' (5:17, NIV).

Now that Job has broken the silence, his friends are ready to say their piece. Each one speaks in turn, with Job responding after each speech. Each of them speaks some element of the truth, but these friends, for all their wisdom and knowledge, do not know everything. Above all, they do not know the reasons why God has allowed the accuser to buffet and test Job. Their analysis is thus flawed from the beginning.

Eliphaz, presumably the oldest, is the first to speak. Having personally observed how God works, Eliphaz claims to be a man of great knowledge (*5:27*) and to speak from his own vast experience (*4:8*). His opening words remind Job of how often he himself has comforted and counselled others who have been afflicted. In a way he is saying, 'Come on, Job, now is the time to practise what you've preached to others.' He counsels Job to be confident that his piety will count with God, that though God is chastening him for some sin, it is for a good purpose (*5:17*) and he can be assured that God will not destroy him along with the wicked.

As far as Eliphaz is concerned, the issues are quite clear:

- A good and innocent person never suffers.
- Those who suffer are being punished for their past sins.
- Job's sufferings prove that he has done something wrong in God's eyes.
- Job should stop behaving like a fool (see *5:2*) and humble himself. God will then bless him and all will be well again.
- This experience, then, is a great wake-up call, to bring Job back to God.

Maybe the saddest aspect of this man's advice is that he is attempting, as someone who is not suffering, to silence the overwhelming terror and grief of someone who is. His words bring no relief to Job. They are as tasteless as the white of an uncooked egg (see *6:6,7*) or a meal without salt. Job's question 'Why?' remains unanswered.

Lord, when I don't know what to say, help me to keep my mouth firmly shut!

TUESDAY 13 NOVEMBER

Bildad's Bluntness

Job 8:1–7; 20–22

'Your beginnings will seem humble, so prosperous will your future be' (v. 7, NIV).

While Eliphaz, the first of Job's friends, spoke with some respect for Job, the second speaker, Bildad, speaks bluntly. He has listened to Job's response to Eliphaz and his persistence in declaring his righteousness. He has heard Job's doubt expressed to God about the value of living a righteous life, and his conclusion that he would be better off dead.

A great head of steam builds for Bildad as he listens, so that when he does speak, it is with impatience. He accuses Job of speaking 'blustering wind' (*v. 2*), or in the Hebrew 'mighty wind', a sad reminder of the great wind that destroyed the house of his oldest son and all his children (*1:19*). Bildad claims that the heart of the matter is God's justice. God cannot be unjust, and God would not punish a just man, therefore Job must be unjust. What's more, Job's children obviously died as a result of their own wickedness (*v. 4*). Job himself must have sinned, for how else could he account for his catastrophic losses and his dreadful skin disease? The only difference is that God has not taken Job's life, indicating that Job's sin is less serious than that of his children.

But that is not Bildad's main concern. Like Eliphaz, he wants to advise Job about the conditions for his future restoration. Job must do two things. First, he must approach God in a spirit of true piety, imploring God's favour (*v. 5*). Second, he must be morally pure and upright (*v. 6*). Bildad concludes his description of Job's restoration by contrasting the past and future and appealing to the accumulated wisdom of tradition, the only place of security.

Once again, as readers privy to the heavenly dialogue in chapter 1, we know something that Bildad does not. And having peeked at the last chapter, we know that God will bless Job's future even more than his past (*vv. 7,21*). Bildad, for all his pompous certainty and harsh judgments, is at least correct on one count.

Prayer

Lord, let me speak words of blessing, not bluntness, today.

WEDNESDAY 14 NOVEMBER

Zophar's Wisdom

Job 11:1–20

'Can you fathom the mysteries of God? Can you probe the limits of the Almighty?' (v. 7, NIV).

Zophar is the third of Job's friends to speak. Bildad, the previous speaker, was blunt, but Zophar is downright arrogant. Full of anger, he lashes out at Job, saying that Job deserves even more punishment, not less. Zophar takes a similar position as that of Eliphaz (*Job 4–5*) and Bildad (*Job 8*) in telling Job that he is suffering greatly because he has sinned greatly.

He speaks of the height, depth, length and width of God's wisdom (*vv. 8,9*), words which bring to mind Paul's description of Christ's love (see *Eph 3:18*). God's wisdom, says Zophar, is greater than the reaches of the cosmos, and Job in his finite smallness cannot possibly search out its vastness. He applies to Job a proverb about the unlikelihood of a witless or empty-headed person finding wisdom. Calling Job an ass for not understanding what is so obvious to Zophar himself, he appeals to Job to take the steps that will restore his hope and security. Job needs to reorder his life – heart, hands, face (*vv. 13–15*) – in harmony with the order of God's world, and evict any form of deceit from his home (*v. 14*).

As certain as Zophar is that Job is guilty, Job is just as certain that he is innocent. As certain as Job is that he knows the truth about himself, Zophar is just as certain that only God can know such a thing. For Zophar, truth lies in the hidden things of knowledge, the mysteries of God's ways, which no human can grasp. For Job, truth can and must be open to scrutiny, as in a trial.

The two men thus face each other, with unresolvable issues between them. Zophar claims to speak with God's wisdom but Job wishes that he and his friends would just be silent. In Job's eyes, that would be wisdom indeed (see *13:5*)!

To pray

There is a time to be silent and a time to speak (Eccl 3:7). Lord, give me the wisdom to know the time today!

THURSDAY 15 NOVEMBER

Job's Distress

Job 19:23–29

'I know that my Redeemer lives, and that in the end he will stand upon the earth. And after my skin has been destroyed, yet in my flesh I will see God' (vv. 25,26, NIV).

Job has listened to each of his three friends make their impassioned speeches. 'You are the people,' he says sarcastically, 'and wisdom will die with you' (*12:2*). He calls them 'miserable comforters' (*16:2*), 'worthless physicians' (*13:4*) who smear him with lies rather than with healing balm. He acknowledges that many of their ideas about God are true, that he is just and that he punishes sin. But they are wrong to assume that Job's suffering is punishment for his sins. Even more painful for Job than their harsh judgments, however, is God's silence and apparent rejection. Job begs God to withdraw his terrors and torment and to start communicating with him (*13:21–25*).

Life is brief and full of trouble, he groans (*14:1*). All that has happened to him – loss, sickness and loneliness – give him no other conclusion than that life is unfair. His children have died, his wife and family find him repulsive (*19:17*), his friends condemn him, and now even God in his anger has deserted him. 'If only you would hide me in the grave and conceal me till your anger has passed!' (*14:13*). Once more the friends respond to Job's laments. A new round of talks repeats the old themes, but this time with even greater impatience and insinuation.

At the very heart of the book, at his lowest point, Job suddenly cries out a ringing affirmation of confidence: 'I know that my Redeemer lives' (*19:25*). Having called God his opponent and tormentor, Job here expresses his confidence that ultimately God will defend and vindicate him against all the false accusations of his so-called friends. The ravages of his disease will inevitably bring about his death, but he is absolutely certain that death is not the end of his existence and that one day he will see his Redeemer with his own eyes (*19:27; cf. 1 John 3:2*). 'He knows the way that I take; when he has tested me, I shall come forth as gold' (*23:10*).

To reflect on

Job still does not know 'why'. But he does know 'who'.

FRIDAY 16 NOVEMBER

Call to Repentance

Job 22:21–30

'Submit to God and be at peace with him; in this way prosperity will come to you' (v. 21, NIV).

It would be easy to dismiss all that Job's friends say as so much hot air – the kind of accusation they make about him, in fact (see *15:2–3*). But now and again a gem of truth shines through the dross of what they say. One such example is the beautiful summary of repentance that Eliphaz makes in chapter 22.

He is wrong in using these words to tell Job what he needs to do, for his judgment is based on his assumptions that Job is a very wicked man (as evidenced by his great suffering) and that his major concern is the return of his prosperity (see *v. 21*). Job has made it quite clear that his greatest longing is to see God and to have their friendship restored (*19:25–27*).

But for all his false conclusions, Eliphaz speaks in these verses with eloquence as he describes the process of repentance:

- Submit to God.
- Lay up God's words in your heart.
- Return to the Almighty and forsake wickedness.
- Find your delight in God.
- Pray and obey.
- Become concerned with sinners.

Eliphaz's vision is of a gracious God, always ready to receive the repentant. Job needs to reorder his life according to God's teaching and to evict wickedness from his home and his values. Eliphaz paints a picture of Job actually returning gold to the places from which it was dug, and taking God as his gold and silver instead. Returning gold to the far-away, legendary land of Ophir would be an extravagant gesture. Yet Job would receive something far more valuable than what he parted with, and this would more than repay his efforts.

The result of such an action will be a transformation of Job's relationship with God, from alienation to trust. Just as sin makes people hang their heads in shame, so repentance enables them to lift their faces to God in prayer, thus restoring the intimacy between them.

To reflect on

When it comes to repentance, we need to turn back in order to move forward.

SATURDAY 17 NOVEMBER

Job's Closing Discourse

Job 27:1–12

'As long as I have life within me, the breath of God in my nostrils, my lips will not speak wickedness, and my tongue will utter no deceit' (vv. 3,4, NIV).

Job's speech in response to his friends takes up the next six chapters. He begins by brushing off Bildad's latest reply (*Job 25*) as irrelevant and tells his friends that, contrary to their own claim, they cannot possibly know everything about God.

He then stands like a lawyer giving his final summing-up of his case. First he looks back with some nostalgia and reviews his former happiness, wealth and honour (*Job 29*). With a great deal of emotion he recalls 'the days when God watched over me, when his lamp shone upon my head . . . when God's intimate friendship blessed my house, when the Almighty was still with me' (*vv. 2–5*). Cream and olive oil (*v. 6*), symbols of richness and luxury, were in abundance then. He was a public figure, a valued and respected city elder. 'I rescued . . . I made the widow's heart sing . . . I was eyes to the blind and feet to the lame. I was a father to the needy.' He thought that life would always be like that, rich and full of blessing (*v. 18*).

'But now . . .' (*30:1*) everything is different. He bemoans the suffering and dishonour that have come upon him. Young and old who once deferred to him now mock him. His bow that was once ever new and strong (*29:20*) has been unstrung. God has overwhelmed him with snares, terrors, suffering, gnawing pains, inner churning. 'My harp is tuned to mourning, and my flute to the sound of wailing' (*30:31*).

Finally, he lists all the sins he has not committed, neither in his heart nor in action. Sexual lust, cheating in business, marital infidelity – he is innocent of them all. He calls for a curse on his land if he has not been fully committed to social justice (*31:38–40*). In strong legal terms Job completes his defence. He puts his signature to the document (*v. 35*). There is nothing more to be said. The matter of his innocence now rests with God.

To reflect on

Job's theme throughout has been: 'Though he slay me, yet will I hope in him' (13:15).

SUNDAY 18 NOVEMBER

A Prayer for Entering God's House

Psalm 26

'I love the house where you live, O LORD, the place where your glory dwells' (v. 8, NIV).

The alarm clock is ignored. Mum and Dad sleep in after having a late night. The kids are up watching cartoons on TV. There's no milk for breakfast. Lost socks, a popped button, dirty shoes all hold up the dressing routine. The chilly morning makes the car hard to start. The family arrives at church ten minutes late, with Dad silent, Mum snappy and the kids squabbling.

Such a scenario certainly makes it difficult to enter into worship. In contrast, Psalm 26 gives us a glimpse of pilgrims arriving at the temple for worship. Psalm 15 asked, 'Who may dwell?' Psalm 24 asked 'Who may ascend?' In Psalm 26 the priest's question is not given, but the words of the psalm form the answer that would be spoken by each worshipper, probably in unison as a group as they stand at the entrance to the temple.

'Vindicate me,' they chant, meaning, 'See if I am worthy to enter your house.' Having invited God's inspection, each worshipper affirms their blameless life. None is claiming to be sinless, but stating that they have lived with both integrity towards others and trust in God. Likening God to a refiner of metal, they invite both God's testing and refining. Constantly aware of God's covenant loving kindness and faithfulness, they have hated and shunned the 'assembly of evildoers' (*v. 5*) as much as they now desire and anticipate 'the great assembly' (*v. 12*) of worshippers in the temple. Each one washes their hands (*v. 6*) in a water font at the temple entrance, a ritual symbolising the inner cleansing of their heart and mind. They recall other occasions when they have come, not to admire the architectural splendour of the building, but to be in the glorious presence of God. 'I love this place,' they declare (*v. 8*).

These worshippers seem to fulfil the 'clean hands and pure heart' requirements of Psalm 24, but when all has been said and done, they know that the final qualification for their admission is God's mercy.

May we come to worship today with a similar spirit!

MONDAY 19 NOVEMBER

Poem on Wisdom

Job 28:1–28

'The fear of the Lord – that is wisdom, and to shun evil is understanding' (v. 28, NIV).

A gem of wisdom shines through the dark lament of Job's final speech. Chapter 28 is like a meditative interlude, a poem on wisdom which is considered one of the most exquisite poetic compositions of the whole Bible. Precious jewels serve as an important image, and the poem itself is like a gemstone, beautifully crafted, clear and luminous, full of mysterious depths.

The first section of the poem describes the place of precious metals – silver, gold, iron and copper – and the heroic human search in remote places to obtain them from the deepest mines. Even wide-ranging animals and keen-eyed birds are ignorant of where precious metals are to be found, but people are skilled in locating and mining them and bringing them to the surface of the earth.

There is a site where silver can be found and a place for gold, but where can wisdom be found, and where is the place of understanding? Again the image of precious metals is used to make the comparison. One cannot buy wisdom for all the precious metals and jewels in the world. Onyx, sapphire, crystal, coral, jasper, rubies and topaz – all the fabled riches from widely differing places in the world cannot compare with, or be exchanged for, wisdom.

So where does wisdom come from? Eliphaz claimed it could be learned only by first-hand experience of life. Bildad believed it is inherited from the past. Zophar saw wisdom as coming from the wise, and cited himself as an example. But God 'understands the way to it and he alone knows where it dwells' (*v. 23*). It cannot be mined or purchased. God alone is the answer to the mystery that Job and his friends have sought to fathom.

Proverbs 8 echoes this chapter on wisdom. There, too, wisdom is displayed as precious and beyond compare. Wisdom was the first of God's creative acts and the craftsman at his side (*v. 30*) when he created the world.

To reflect on

Wisdom's call to believers today is to listen, to watch, to wait and to find life in God (Proverbs 8:34,35).

TUESDAY 20 NOVEMBER

Elihu's Arrogance

Job 32:1–22

'My words come from an upright heart; my lips sincerely speak what I know' (33:3, NIV).

When Job's three friends first came to see him (*Job 2*), they were silenced at the sight of his devastating illness and overwhelming grief. At the end of Job's long speech (*Job 26–31*), they are once more silenced, this time because they see him as 'righteous in his own eyes'. While this is true, Job's friends consider him a fool, and having told him so, they now have nothing more to say.

At this point a young man, Elihu, steps forward. He may have been respectfully listening to the long discourses, or his words may be a later addition to the book. Unlike the other friends, this one has an Israelite name, and he addresses Job by name. He describes himself 'like bottled-up wine, like new wineskins ready to burst'. And burst he does, first with angry words directed at Job for his declared innocence, and then at the three friends who, he believes, have failed to correct Job's wrong thinking. He has listened to age speak; now he declares that true wisdom will speak (see *36:4*).

Elihu says that he is offended by Job's claim to purity (*33:9*) and by his complaints about God's silence in the face of his terrible suffering (*33:13*). Elihu insists that God does indeed speak, in dreams and visions, through suffering and illness and by mediating angels who take men's sacrifices to God.

Job had complained that God terrified him with dreams and visions (*7:13–14*) but Elihu claims that these would be God's attempt to warn him and thus save his life. Job has seen his illness and suffering as a sign of God's enmity and desire to humiliate him (*30:16–19*), but Elihu sees it as God's chastening. What Job has suffered as rejection, Elihu claims is redemption. While Job has endured God's punishment and asked 'Why?', Elihu suggests that he should receive it as God's presence and say 'Thank you'.

At the end of a speech full of closed dogmatism and damning judgment, the stage is set for the true voice of wisdom.

Prayer

Lord, please guard my words today!

WEDNESDAY 21 NOVEMBER

God Speaks

Job 38:1–21

'The LORD said to Job: "Will the one who contends with the Almighty correct him? Let him who accuses God answer him!" ' (40:1,2, NIV).

From the midst of the whirlwind, God speaks. Surprisingly, he does not answer any of Job's questions. He says nothing about Job's suffering, nor does he address Job's problem about divine justice. Job is declared neither guilty nor innocent. God states that Job's complaining and raging against him are unjustified and come from his limited understanding. He then proceeds to ply Job with rhetorical questions, to each of which Job must plead ignorance.

When the earth was created, the angels were there to sing the praises of the Creator, but Job was not. He should therefore not expect to be able to understand even lesser aspects of God's plans. Inanimate creation, the great deep, the underworld, the expanse of the earth and the heavens all testify to God's sovereignty and power. He can command and unleash or restrain them at will. If Job cannot explain the earth's natural order, how could he possibly explain God's moral order?

In like manner, animal creation – the lion, raven, mountain goat, wild donkey, wild ox, ostrich, horse, hawk and eagle – all testify to God's sovereignty, power and loving care. Does Job know how any of them exist? Did he give wisdom to the lion to hunt, the hawk to fly, the eagle to soar, the raven to find food, the mountain goat to give birth? Hearing this great panorama of the cosmos, Job is chastened and humbled. He is no longer 'like a prince' (*31:37*), and submits to God's power and sovereignty.

God continues, speaking of his justice and Job's futile efforts at self-justification. Job is urged to leave all the matters of justice, including his own vindication, in God's strong hands. God created and can care for and control the mighty behemoth (a large land animal such as an elephant or hippopotamus) and leviathan (a large aquatic animal, probably a crocodile), which means that he is even greater than these.

To reflect on

God's questions, 'Who is this . . . ?' 'Where were you . . . ?' 'Are you able . . . ?' lift Job from his dust heap to a much greater perspective.

THURSDAY 22 NOVEMBER

Job's New Perspective

Job 40:3–5; 42:1–6

'My ears had heard of you but now my eyes have seen you' (42:5, NIV).

At the beginning of Job's story the accuser had predicted that once he was deprived of his family, possessions and health, Job would curse God (*1:11; 2:5*). But Job does not. Immediately following God's speech concerning behemoth and leviathan, Job replies. He acknowledges God's power and accepts God's judgment that Job has spoken without understanding. It is as if Job has gained a new perspective on himself and his suffering, seeing himself now as God sees him.

As a wealthy and successful father, landowner and civic leader, Job's life showed all the accepted signs of divine blessing. His experience of life was ordered and fair, black and white with no shades of grey. Good things happened to good people, bad things happened to bad people. So when his unexpected and overwhelming suffering happened, he declared the disaster morally wrong and unjustified, and looked for someone to blame. If only God would give him an audience, he would find an answer to his question 'Why?'

His suffering plunged him into a great abyss of chaos, despair and isolation, where all the usual ordered things were turned upside down. 'What I feared has come upon me; what I dreaded has happened to me' (*3:25*). He had become 'a brother of jackals, a companion of owls' (*30:29*). His life was like a desolate wasteland.

God's speeches reminded Job of the establishment of the earth on secure foundations, the reliable return of the dawn each day, the regulation of life-giving water and the daily nurture of animals. God described a world that is rich in goodness and where chaos (symbolised by leviathan) is present but contained within secure boundaries. Pain can be neither avoided nor abolished, for it is part of the fabric of life. But just as God satisfies even the desolate wasteland with rain, so there is no place or condition which is beyond the sustaining power of God's presence.

To reflect on

Do you know someone who lives in an inner 'desolate wasteland'? Find some way of telling that person today that God looks on them as his child.

FRIDAY 23 NOVEMBER

God's Verdict

Job 42:7–9

'After the LORD had said these things to Job, he said to Eliphaz the Temanite, "I am angry with you and your two friends, because you have not spoken of me what is right, as my servant Job has" ' (v. 7, NIV).

Following Job's reply to God, the voice of the narrator takes up the story and brings it to a conclusion. First, God rebukes Job's three friends for not speaking what is right, as Job has done. It is hard to reconcile this with God's recent rebuke to Job for having spoken 'words without knowledge' (*38:2*). The word 'right' means 'correct'. Job's sincerity is not in question here. The story line has shown him to be a hero of unconditional piety who never wavers in his commitment despite extraordinary and inexplicable adversity.

The words of the friends, however, for all the shreds of truth they contained, are now dismissed as folly (*v. 8*). Their spiritual arrogance had caused them to claim wisdom they did not in fact possess. They are silenced by God's rebuke.

Having been tested and proved faithful, it seems only fitting that Job should emerge as the hero, and his friends be shown up as the villains of the piece. In an expression of generosity, the story ends with even the rebuked friends being restored. Just as Job had acted as priest for his children (*1:5*), now he acts as intercessor on behalf of his friends. The demand that they sacrifice seven bulls and seven rams seems excessive, but it is in keeping with the symbolic numbers of the first chapter. Their sacrifice and Job's prayer serve to reconcile them with God.

The most tender aspect of these verses is the way that God speaks to the friends about 'my servant Job'. Job's words may not have been correct, but he is still God's valued servant. This expression is used four times in two verses and recalls God's assessment to the accuser that there was no one on earth like 'my servant Job' (*1:8*). In spite of all his inexplicable sufferings and the apparent dark absence of God, Job emerges at the end of the story still a friend of God, in intimate relationship with him.

To reflect on

Servant and friend – both aspects were part of Job's relationship with God. Can the same be said about you?

SATURDAY 24 NOVEMBER

Job's Restoration

Job 42:10–17

'After Job had prayed for his friends, the LORD made him prosperous again and gave him twice as much as he had before' (v. 10, NIV).

God has spoken, Job has repented, his friends are reconciled. The story concludes with a 'happy ever after' ending. Job's family and friends come to share a meal with him and to offer gestures of comfort, each one giving him a piece of silver and a gold ring. The support of Job's brothers and sisters in his sorrow echoes the joyful birthday celebrations shown by his children, the brothers and sisters of the first chapter. The significant gifts they bring will, under God's blessing, become the enormous fortune he enjoys in the latter part of his life.

His animal herds are restored, twice as many as he had at the beginning, and a new family of seven sons and three daughters is born to him. The remarkable number of sons is matched by the remarkable beauty of his daughters. Their names reinforce the picture of their beauty. Job gives them an inheritance along with their brothers. The final indication of Job's blessedness lies in the length of life granted to him. The years of his life after his calamity are the equivalent of two normal lifetimes, in which he sees four generations of his descendants. Finally he dies, 'old and full of days'.

On one hand, such a happy ending seems fitting. Job's story is a journey that ends tidily where it began. But on the other hand, this ending has a somewhat teasing, uncomfortable quality, not unlike some of Jesus' parables. Children who die tragically cannot just be 'replaced' with new ones.

Job's story has presented a community of voices struggling to make sense of suffering. Each voice has valid insights as well as blindness to other aspects of the problem. Job found a new perspective on the meaning of his life and suffering, and finally a sense of peace as he wrestled with God. He found no final answer to his question 'Why?' But in listening to the voice from the whirlwind he did find an answer to his question 'Who?'

May it be so for you today as well.

SUNDAY 25 NOVEMBER

A Royal Declaration

Psalm 27

'One thing I ask of the LORD, this is what I seek: that I may dwell in the house of the LORD all the days of my life, to gaze upon the beauty of the LORD and to seek him in his temple' (v. 4, NIV).

The setting for Psalm 27 may well be a royal event such as the anniversary of a coronation. God's covenant with David was eternal (see *2 Sam 7:16*), but it was also renewed in the coronation of every new monarch. Annually the king would restate his coronation commitments, and he would not depart for war without first consulting God and offering sacrifices and prayer. Psalm 27 is both a declaration of confidence in God and a prayer for divine aid. The psalmist may be a king, but he is also a son, humbly aware of his need of his father's help:

- He declares that the Lord is his light. Whether it is the dark valley of death that throws terrifying shadows upon his way, or the military dangers that he faces, he has no fear, for God is the light that dispels such darkness.
- He declares that the Lord is his salvation. No matter how great the military odds against him, he knows that God will give victory and deliverance.
- He declares that the Lord is his refuge, a place of safety even in the midst of battle.
- He declares that he longs to live in the house of the Lord, not as a temple servant, but living permanently in God's presence. Being delivered from military threats will make it possible for him to dwell in God's house, just as his faith, renewed in God's house, will give him fearlessness in the face of military threats.

'Now my head is lifted up,' he says (*v. 6*). Having made his declarations, he now makes his sacrifices and then his prayer. He prays to God for there is no one else to whom he can turn. He asks to be instructed to walk in God's way, and to be delivered from those who oppose him. The psalm concludes with his statement of confidence (*v. 13*) and the priest's encouragement for him to wait, with both strength and courage, for God's help that will surely come.

Let the confident declarations of this psalm be your prayer today.

A BOWL OF FRUIT

Introduction

A bowl of fruit sits invitingly on my kitchen bench. Bright-skinned mandarins, ripe bananas, soft-fleshed tamarillos, crunchy Pacific Rose apples, furry-skinned kiwifruit (recently renamed zespri). The full bowl is a picture of colour and nourishment, a focal centre of welcome in the room.

When I read Paul's list of the fruit of the Spirit in Galatians 5:22, it reminds me of a bowl of fruit like the one in my kitchen. Paul wrote this list to the Christians in Galatia who were engaged in a battle of ideas that threatened to turn faith into legalism and rule-keeping. Paul's great cry was 'Freedom!' and he painted his freedom banner with the bright colours of love, joy, peace, patience, kindness, goodness, faithfulness, gentleness and self-control. These are the qualities, he said, that give evidence of God's Holy Spirit at work in your lives.

I see such evidence in the lives of people I know – a man of gentleness, a woman who bubbles over with joy, a friend who characterises patience, someone else who is the epitome of faithfulness. It is my pleasure to introduce you to these friends in this brief series, with the hope that you too will allow God to cultivate the fruit of the Spirit in your life.

MONDAY 26 NOVEMBER

Love

Matthew 25:31–40

'The fruit of the Spirit is . . . love' (Gal 5:22, NIV).

I know a man who seems to be full of love. He told me that he learned to love in a very unlikely place – a beggar's camp in the heart of India. Dave had grown up in a loving family and always had a gentle disposition, but a new experience of learning to love began when he and his wife, Shirley, left for India as missionaries in the early 1960s. For over five years they worked at a home for the destitute in Bombay.

The home incorporated a beggar's camp for 200 men prisoners and 100 old and disabled women, and a workshop for seventy boys, some of whom were prisoners waiting for job rehabilitation. At the workshop the boys made cardboard boxes, rewired motors and assembled plastic flowers and mosaic tiles. On the same compound there was a 100-bed hospital. For Dave and Shirley's three young children, this compound was their first home.

'It was in that place,' says Dave, 'that I saw people who needed love and I learned to love them. They were so poor, but they were still people of dignity. They taught me about themselves, but even more about Christ. I saw his character in their eyes.' Even today, more than thirty years later, Dave speaks of his great debt to those poor people. 'They had nothing, but I met Jesus, in them. That beggar's camp became holy ground.'

Shirley died in India after a very brief illness. Dave eventually returned to his homeland with his children who were still young, not yet in their teens. The love that he found in that unlikely place, and the God who gave it, carried him and his family through a deep experience of loss and back into new ministry back home. Still today, Dave lives 'for those who need love'.

To reflect on

Love doesn't need a full purse or great expertise. It simply needs an unfailing source and a channel to pour through. Let God's unfailing supply of love flow through the channel of your life today.

TUESDAY 27 NOVEMBER

Joy

Galatians 5:16–26

'The fruit of the Spirit is . . . joy' (v. 22, NIV).

I met a woman recently who overflowed with joy. She was irrepressible. Joy bubbled out of her like an overflowing glass of lemonade. She smiled as she spoke and her eyes danced with delight. Her laugh had an infectious quality that drew me in and warmed the sad places of my heart. I thought, 'Here is a truly joyful woman. Everything in her life must be good.' I wanted to get to know her better, call her my friend, catch some of the joy she had to spare.

A few days later, I had opportunity to talk with her alone. As she told me her story, her eyes still danced, but there was a wistful sadness in her smile. She told me about her husband who is not a Christian and about the heavy burden of depression she often carries. This joyful woman depressed? Surely not!

Our conversation reminded me of two things. To begin with, first impressions may be accurate, but they are only surface. As we get to know people, a fuller picture with both light and shade emerges. Secondly, happiness depends on happenings, but joy comes from a much deeper place down in the heart somewhere. It's a place deeper than circumstances, deeper than mood swings, deeper than heavy loads. In that deep place, God meets with us, every day if we are willing, touching our lives with his peace, lifting our spirit, hoisting the other end of our load onto his strong shoulders.

Even as Jesus faced the cross, he spoke to his disciples about joy. 'I have told you this so that my joy may be in you and that your joy may be complete' (*John 15:11*). 'Ask and you will receive, and your joy will be complete' (*John 16:24*). Dreary Christianity? A joyless believer? Such expressions are surely contradictions. God welcomes us to a life characterised by deep joy, no matter what our outward circumstances may be.

To reflect on

Like my new friend, I'm lifting my heart to God today, and asking for his joy. Will you join me?

WEDNESDAY 28 NOVEMBER

Patience

1 Peter 5:6–11

'The fruit of the Spirit is . . . patience' (Gal 5:22, NIV).

I know a man of patience. Not the 'I'm waiting for the water to boil' kind of patience, but a creative and redemptive endurance that is enabling him to turn loss into life.

He was a man of stature in every sense – tall, commanding, in a top leadership position when, in a moment as sudden as a braking vehicle and a breaking neck, everything changed. The accident left him paralysed from the neck down, a tetraplegic. There followed dark days of devastation, weeks of intensive care, months of rehabilitation, years of learning how to make a 'new normal' out of life.

Travelling a long, deep valley of grief, he had to let go of many things he had carried lightly – the ability to sing, to help with household chores, to handwrite a letter. These days he's confined to a wheelchair and dependent upon others for his very existence. He cannot bounce his latest grandchild on his knee, nor play the piano or cello, nor even comb his own hair.

But you would search in vain to find self-pity or impatience joy-riding on his wheelchair. Rather than lamenting what he has lost, this man is squeezing the juice out of every day. His eyes, ears and voice now make up his life. He has trained as a spiritual director and offers the gift of listening and prayer to others. With the help of a voice-activated computer he keeps in touch with friends and family around the world and with missionaries in far-flung places. Through the Internet he fields questions about Christian ethics and practice and gives considered responses that help people hear the voice of God more clearly. His mission field now comes to him daily in the form of carers, most of whom are Asian medical students.

The promise that God will one day 'restore you and make you strong' (*1 Pet 5:10*) keeps him pressing on. One day, in God's time, he knows that everything will be made perfect. For that day he works, and waits, with patience.

To reflect on

What do you wait for with patience?

THURSDAY 29 NOVEMBER

Faithfulness

Galatians 5:22–26

'Charm is deceptive, and beauty is fleeting; but a woman who fears the LORD is to be praised' (Prov 31:30, NIV).

When I think of faithfulness, I think of a woman whom my husband and I first met when we were appointed to a small corps for our second year of training as officers. We were welcomed by this woman as an answer to prayer, which is a great way to begin!

She was single, a Salvation Army officer about to retire. The corps was small and struggling and under constant threat of closure. But this woman and her friend, another single woman, were not about to let that happen. Imagine these two women on their knees in fervent prayer, pleading with God to send them three men! They saw men, holy and hard-working, as key to the corps' survival. Hence the delight when my husband and I arrived. At least one third of their prayer was answered and, within a short time, two more men arrived.

This woman was diminutive and not strong physically, but she had grit and determination, as well as a sense of humour that at times rescued her and at other times got her into trouble! She became a mentor for me, long before I knew what a mentor was, and she loved my children, a sure way to any parent's heart.

Every week during Sunday school she took a youngster with learning difficulties through the lesson. Every year she wrote and produced a drama. Everyone in the corps had a part. She rehearsed, sewed costumes, made props and delighted at how God blessed it all.

She told me one day of a senior leader who had scolded her in one appointment because her corps' statistics were not showing seekers at the mercy seat every week. She responded, 'Sir, if every day I offer to God everything I do and every person I meet and every conversation I have, what more can I do?'

That's how this woman lived her calling. She invited God into every part of her life, then lived him out to all around her, with joy, with love and with faithfulness.

To reflect on

Could the word 'faithful' describe you?

FRIDAY 30 NOVEMBER

Gentleness

1 Timothy 3:1–7

'. . . not violent but gentle . . .' (v. 3, NIV).

He's a giant of a man, over six feet tall, with huge feet and hands, and a disarming white smile that lights up his dark face. Back home in Fiji, Joe would melt into the crowd, but in the neighbourhood where he now lives, everything about him stands out. For all his size, Joe has a gentle spirit. His manner is gentle, he walks gently and holds out gentle hands in welcome to all whom he meets.

It was not always like that. In his younger years, Joe was into trouble, big time. He was the typical rebellious youth who left the covering of his praying parents to look for life. He found it, or thought he did, in drugs and alcohol. In the 1987 coup in Fiji, he was on the side of the rebels, paid to burn down shops and terrorise people.

But a turning point came. One day Joe's mother sat him down and asked, 'When are you going to come back to the truth you were taught as a child?' It was a well-practised question, for each of Joe's five brothers had walked away from the loving environment in which they grew up.

Joe says that, in that moment, he knew his mother spoke truth, and that he had to change the direction of his life. One by one, each of his brothers came home, thanks to their mother's persistent prayers. In some ways, this could be her story. A faithful woman, she knew enough of the deep love of God to not give up loving and praying and waiting for her prodigal family.

Joe walked away that day from the drug crop he was growing, away from the alcohol and from his drinking friends. He became involved in the local Salvation Army corps as a youth leader and an evangelism visitor. These days, he is preparing for training as a Salvation Army officer. He's single-minded, determined, fearless, but above all, gentle, with the love of a Father God who has never let him go.

To reflect on

Gentleness is strength under control.

HE COMES SINGING LOVE

Introduction

Today, the first day of December, is the beginning of the season of Advent. This is the season of hope and wonder, the season of waiting and watching. Like a child waiting for a birthday, or with nose pressed against the window waiting for someone to arrive, we stand on tiptoe. We eagerly wait for the birth of the baby whose coming we celebrate at Christmas. As we wait, we look back and reflect on some of the promises that were given concerning his coming. We look to see his presence in our midst today, God's 'with-us-ness'. We recognise that it is with love, with mercy and forgiveness, and at great cost that he comes.

These meditations are like an Advent calendar which, beginning today, opens on one scene after another of the Christmas story. The story may be very familiar to us but, like a child with a favourite book, we need to hear it again and again, for it is a story of real people caught up in a life-changing drama that somehow wonderfully enfolds us as well.

Join with me as we stand on tiptoe together in this time of waiting and watching, then as we celebrate his coming. Let us rejoice once again that 'a Saviour is born to us, who is Christ the Lord!'

Come, thou long-expected Jesus,
Born to set thy people free;
From our fears and sins release us,
Let us find our rest in thee.
Charles Wesley, SASB 79

SATURDAY 1 DECEMBER

Waiting for His Coming

Romans 8:18–25

'. . . if we hope for what we do not yet have, we wait for it patiently' (v. 25, NIV).

So much of life is waiting. We wait for babies to be born and frail loved ones to die. We wait for pizzas in fast-food outlets and for postage stamps in slow queues. We wait at traffic lights and hospital bedsides, for appointments and anniversaries, for water to boil and grass to grow, for meals to cook and wounds to heal.

All of life, it seems, has an element of vigil – waiting with watchfulness. The season of Advent is the season of vigil but it's harder than at any other time of the year, because this Advent vigil is best kept with a still heart. That's difficult when there is so much to do – greetings to send, gifts to purchase, food to organise, holiday plans to finalise, events to attend, endless lists to make and then obey. It may seem impossible to find a still place where we can be with God and listen. Impossible? No. Difficult? Certainly. But essential if we are to avoid arriving at Christmas Day all prepared but exhausted, dished up on the outside and dried up on the inside.

God's invitation to us in these next few weeks is to come aside and be still in his presence. Look for God's stillness in your own home – in the darkened room where your child sleeps peacefully at night, or in the gentle light of a new day. Listen to God's stillness as you go outside and welcome the first snow of the season gently falling, or the first flowers of the pohutukawa tree.

This is the time of waiting for the fulfilment of the promise, conceived in the heart of God, declared from the beginning of time, given at a specific moment in history, and still coming at a time that is yet to be. We kneel to celebrate God's plan of salvation, wrapped up in the person of Jesus. At the same time, we stand on tiptoe, waiting for the fullness of his coming, the freedom and redemption of ourselves and all of creation.

Prayer

Lord, I welcome you and I wait for you.

SUNDAY 2 DECEMBER
First Sunday in Advent

Isaiah 9:2–7

'For to us a child is born, to us a son is given, and the government will be on his shoulders. And he will be called Wonderful Counsellor, Mighty God, Everlasting Father, Prince of Peace' (v. 6, NIV).

Today is the first Sunday in Advent. Many churches around the world celebrate the four Sundays leading up to Christmas by progressively lighting the candles on an Advent wreath. The wreath is in the shape of a circle – symbol of God's unending love. It often has a large white 'Christ candle' in the centre, surrounded by three purple candles and one that is rose coloured. Today the first purple candle, representing hope, is lit.

The coming of Christ was anchored in the promises of the Old Testament, many of which are found in the book of Isaiah, written some 700 years earlier. Isaiah had a tough task, calling the people of Judah, Israel and the surrounding heathen nations to turn from their sins and back to God. He urged them to return, repent and be renewed, and spoke the promise of God's redemption, which would be a cause of rejoicing for all.

He wrote the promise of a child being born who would shatter the darkness of sin and bring light to all living in the shadow of death. This child would be the Messiah, a royal son of David, whose names would give insight into his nature. He would be called Wonderful Counsellor, for he would carry out a royal plan that would cause the entire world to marvel. He would be called Mighty God, for he would have divine power to make the impossible possible. He would be called Everlasting Father, for he would be an enduring, compassionate provider and protector. He would be called Prince of Peace, for his rule would bring an end to hostility and hatred.

To our world grown hopeless and needing hope now more than ever, this child is promised once again. We stand on tiptoe and watch and wait for his coming. Pray today for someone you know who has lost hope, that God will light a candle of hope in their heart.

Christ will come – we watch.
Christ is coming – we wait.
Christ is here – we worship.
Christ will come again – we watch and wait and worship.

MONDAY 3 DECEMBER

Watching for His Coming

Habakkuk 2:1–3

'I will stand at my watch and station myself on the ramparts;
I will look to see what he will say to me . . .' (v. 1, NIV).

Advent is the season of watching. If we are not careful, all we will see is the commercialism of the season, the cheap wrappings, the monsters that grab us by the shoulders and urge us to 'Buy, buy, buy!' All we will hear are the familiar readings and the well-worn carols.

But there is a watching that is deeper than seeing, and a hearing more acute than what our ears pick up. In order to really see and hear the Christmas message this year, we may have to get close enough to a child to watch the events through young eyes and ears that have not been tainted with familiarity.

An art teacher set her class of eight-year-olds the task of painting angels. As she passed one boy's table she saw that he had drawn rows of curved lines, like a breeze blowing through someone's hair or willow trees in the wind. They were orderly, unmistakably clear and beautifully simple. The girl sitting next to him noticed and started mocking his picture. Suddenly all the others in the class were laughing that he did not know what an angel looked like. The boy quickly turned his paper over and painted something drearily familiar with wings and a long dress. 'But,' said the teacher, 'I couldn't help wondering whether he knew something I didn't know.'

Many Old Testament Scriptures spoke of the need to watch for a future day of glory. 'The glory of the Lord will be revealed, and all mankind together will see it' (*Isa 40:5*). Jesus himself urged his followers to watch and stay awake for his coming (see *Matt 24:42, 25:13*).

As we scan the Advent horizon, watching for signs of his coming again into our midst, may it be with eyes wide open and the ears of our heart attentive. It may be with surprise, in an unexpected moment, or in an unlikely person that he comes. It may be in the whirl of a busy shopping mall or softly, with the gentle rustle of gossamer wings. But come he will.

Prayer

Lord, I'm watching!

TUESDAY 4 DECEMBER

He Comes – In Justice and Righteousness

Jeremiah 33:12–26

'In those days and at that time I will make a righteous Branch sprout from David's line; he will do what is just and right in the land' (v. 15, NIV).

Today as I write, I look out onto a clear, cloudless sunny morning following a very heavy frost. The blackbirds which usually splash their morning wash in a puddle of water outside my office window will today have to wait until the sun melts the ice cover. The oak trees stand bare in the sun but close inspection reveals signs of spring. It's hard to believe on such a tranquil morning that in many parts of the world tragedy and tension fill the air – continued unrest in Fiji, new waves of starvation in parts of Africa, ongoing conflict in Northern Ireland.

The prophet Jeremiah looked out on dark mornings every day of his forty years as God's spokesman. When Jeremiah spoke, nobody listened. When he condemned sin, nobody cared. When he begged the people to repent, nobody responded. The book of Jeremiah is a dark collection of prophecies about Israel and Judah. God's people will be taken into exile in Babylon; their promised land will be reduced to a desolate wasteland; the city of Jerusalem will be destroyed.

But in the midst of the gloom, a light shines brightly. God promises his people that, in spite of the destruction, they will be restored. His covenant still stands as sure and certain as night follows day. Abraham's descendants will yet be 'as countless as the stars of the sky and as measureless as the sand on the seashore' (*v. 22*). The priestly and royal covenants made with the Levites and with King David will be fulfilled for all time by a righteous Branch sprouting from David's line. In this person, Jesus, God promises that justice and righteousness will fill the whole earth.

In these days of Advent, as we watch for the coming of Christ, let us claim this promise for the entire world. Let us pray for the places where hatreds fester. Let us watch for ways to be part of God's work of healing, peacemaking and reconciliation.

Prayer

God of justice and righteousness, let ____________________ be saved and let ________________ live in safety.

WEDNESDAY 5 DECEMBER

He Comes – To Those in Exile

Jeremiah 29:10–14

'At that time I will gather you; at that time I will bring you home' (Zeph 3:20, NIV).

Advent is the season for coming home. Many sons and daughters of the family turn their hearts towards home at this time of the year. But not everyone can get there. Millions of refugees in our world live as displaced persons in an unfamiliar land with strange food, language and customs, where they have no voice, no vote and no hope of ever returning to the place they once called home.

Their exile finds an echo in the story of the Hebrew people. In Babylon, thousands of people had been taken far from their homeland. Their homes had been burned, the walls of their cities destroyed and their treasures ransacked. As if such geographical exile wasn't bad enough, they were also separated from their religious traditions. It seemed as if God had driven them into exile and abandoned them. 'How can we sing the songs of the LORD while in a foreign land?' they lamented (*Ps 137:4*). Many of them gave up their faith and settled in Babylon, putting down roots into the materialistic and idol-worshipping culture of their new home.

Other Jews remained faithful to God and held a vision of home in their hearts, yearning for the day when they could return. The prophets urged them to hold fast to this hope. The second part of the book of Isaiah calls the exiles in Babylon to come home. Writing to a people who are discouraged and destitute, the author tells of a God who loves them and who longs to save them and bring them home.

Advent cries this strong message of homecoming to all who are in exile, whether geographical and political, or lost in an inner homelessness where we are exiled from ourselves or from those closest to us. Immanuel, God-with-us, offers light, consolation and comfort for our homelessness, promising to resettle us in his love.

Prayer

God of all comfort, help us to reach out to all those exiled in our world and to work for restoration. And when the exile is in our own hearts, please bring us home.

THURSDAY 6 DECEMBER

He Comes – In Restoration

Zephaniah 3:14–20

'The LORD your God is with you, he is mighty to save. He will take great delight in you, he will quiet you with his love, he will rejoice over you with singing' (v. 17, NIV).

The prophet Zephaniah had a task similar to Jeremiah's. As God's spokesman, he was called to speak the truth, even when that meant giving the unwelcome news of judgment and punishment. Zephaniah warned the people of Judah that if they refused to repent and turn from their idols, the entire nation, including Jerusalem, would be lost. He thundered his warning of the day of the Lord that would come. It would be a bitter day of wrath, distress and anguish (*1:14–16*).

But the people were indifferent to Zephaniah's warning. Secure in their prosperity, they no longer cared about God or his demands for righteous living. Zephaniah spoke of God's judgment that would be punishment for their sins. But in the midst of his terrible pronouncement, he whispers a word of hope. 'Seek the Lord... Seek righteousness, seek humility; perhaps you will be sheltered on the day of the Lord's anger' (*2:3*).

That whisper becomes a chant, which grows to a crescendo as God's salvation and deliverance for those who are faithful to him is declared. 'Sing, O Daughter of Zion; shout aloud, O Israel! Be glad and rejoice with all your heart... The LORD has taken away your punishment... never again will you fear any harm' (*3:14,15*). These words of hope are grounded in the knowledge of God's justice and love for his people. Zephaniah sees God, the Holy One of Israel, singing for joy over his people's restoration. He tells them that their lives, as well as their city and their land, will be restored.

Advent is the season of restoration, of hope coming again to people who have grown weary and drained of hope. Watch for signs of God's restoration in these days – an illness healed, a wrong repented and forgiven, a job-training programme giving a new beginning to a once unemployable person, an illiterate adult learning to read, an act of kindness done against a dark background.

Prayer

Faithful God, help me to watch for your moments of restoration, and to hear you singing your song of love over your people.

FRIDAY 7 DECEMBER

He Comes – In Anticipation of Joy

Micah 5:1–5

'A woman giving birth to a child has pain because her time has come; but when her baby is born she forgets the anguish because of her joy that a child is born into the world' (John 16:21, NIV).

The Jewish people were a nation 'in waiting'. They knew the Messiah would come, because he had been promised. But the details of how and when he would come were not so clear.

One image used in Scripture for this experience of waiting is that of a woman anticipating the birth of her baby. It's a very human image – just ask Mary. The Scripture tells us none of the details of her pregnancy. Even doctor Luke fails to mention her puffy ankles, elevated blood pressure or morning sickness. I have a friend, delighted to be pregnant, who declares that morning sickness is a misnomer. For her, it is an all-day event!

The Jewish people knew a similar mix of joy and pain in their waiting. The prophet Micah, living at a time of political unrest, described the judgment of God that was coming upon the nations and the mighty city of Jerusalem. But close by, the little town of Bethlehem would be the birthplace of a king who would save his people. Micah's predictions, hundreds of years earlier, gave the people a promise of hope to hold on to. The whole nation was like a pregnant woman, waiting for her deliverer. The pain and discomfort of waiting would one day be forgotten with the joy of his coming.

Jesus used the same image to describe how his followers would feel once the Holy Spirit had come. Their grief at losing him would be replaced with joy. Paul picked up the same image in his letter to the Galatians, describing himself as a woman 'in the pains of childbirth', waiting for Christ to be formed in them (*Gal 4:19*).

On this very day as I write, I too am anticipating an arrival! This time tomorrow, four little boys – my grandsons – and their parents will be here. The house is ready, the cupboards stocked, library books selected, favourite menus planned. I've waited for months and that's been hard, but now they're coming! Yippee!

Prayer

Lord, thank you for all the joys that lie at the end of our waiting.

SATURDAY 8 DECEMBER

He Comes – With Healing in His Wings

Malachi 4:1–6

'But for you who revere my name, the sun of righteousness will rise with healing in its wings. And you will go out and leap like calves released from the stall' (v. 2, NIV).

Malachi was the last of the Old Testament prophets, writing at a time when the Jewish people had returned from exile in Babylon. The city of Jerusalem and the temple had been rebuilt. The people were well settled once again, their days of exile a fast-fading memory.

But there was complacency in their worship of God. The glorious future announced by the prophets had not yet happened and God had not yet come to his temple with majesty and power (*3:1*). Did God's covenant still stand with his people? Could his justice still be trusted? Such deep and doubting questions were draining the last dregs of hope from the people. To make things worse, the priests, the very ones charged with representing God, were neglecting their task and handling the holy things with contempt.

Into this dark scene, Malachi shines a light of judgment and of hope. The day of the Lord is coming when God will refine his people, like a refiner's fire or launderer's soap (*3:2*). The arrogant will be burned up like stubble at the end of the harvest. But for those who hold fast to God, he will come with saving power and with healing and restoration, as warm and penetrating as the rays of the sun. This day of the Lord will celebrate the coming of the powerful and gentle King of kings. What a day to wait and watch for!

It will be a day of joy. Just as frisky young calves frolic with delight when released from confinement, so the people who revere God's name will kick up their heels in joy, lift their hearts in praise to God, and sing out their hallelujahs! Malachi's prophecy took another 400 years to be fulfilled, but then it was gloriously fulfilled with the coming of Jesus. The warning bells of Malachi's prophecy become the Christmas bells of Matthew's Gospel!

Hail the Heaven-born Prince of Peace!
Hail the Sun of righteousness!
Light and life to all he brings,
Risen with healing in his wings.

Charles Wesley, SASB 82

SUNDAY 9 DECEMBER

Second Sunday in Advent

Isaiah 11:1–10

'The wolf will live with the lamb, the leopard will lie down with the goat, the calf and the lion and the yearling together; and a little child will lead them' (v. 6, NIV).

Today is the second Sunday in Advent and the second purple candle is lit, representing peace, as well as the candle of hope, featured last Sunday. God's light is coming into our darkness.

The Babylonian exile brought the kingdom of Judah to an end. David's kingdom was like a tree that had been felled. But the prophet Isaiah wrote that, from that lifeless stump, a new branch would grow. He would be greater than the original tree and would bear much fruit. He would rule with righteousness, his kingdom characterised by peace. Even animals normally hostile to each other would live at peace. An infant would play unharmed near a cobra or viper. If this would be so in the animal kingdom, then how much more in the world of people?

The story is told of a Christmas Day during World War 1 when men huddled together in the trenches, cold, hungry and homesick. Someone on the British side started singing 'Silent Night, Holy Night', and everyone joined in. At the end of the song there was a pause and then from the German side came the familiar tune with German words, *'Stille Nacht, Heilige Nacht'*. Different language, same meaning. For a gifted moment, the real heart of Christmas was touched.

I write in the wake of the Camp David convention during which the leaders Ehud Barak and Yasser Arafat discussed the complex issues of peace between Israel and Palestine. Sadly, the talks ended with some key issues unresolved. A quick scan of the newspaper indicates that peace is elusive not just for nations, but for neighbours as well. Racial tensions in the suburbs, strife with the neighbours over the fence, brokenness within families – the stories are all too common. How greatly we need to gather together around that humble manger and welcome Jesus, the Prince of Peace, into our midst.

Prayer

Peacemaker Lord, we need your peace in our world, now more than ever. Please light a candle of peace today in the hearts of all who are in strife.

MONDAY 10 DECEMBER

He Comes – In Littleness

Philippians 2:5–11

'But you, Bethlehem Ephrathah, though you are small among the clans of Judah, out of you will come for me one who will be ruler over Israel, whose origins are from of old, from ancient times' (Micah 5:2, NIV).

The prophet Micah, writing hundreds of years before the birth of Jesus, predicted that Israel's deliverer would be born in the small town of Bethlehem in the region of Ephrathah. This detail is the first of many signs that Jesus came in littleness, in humility, in fragility. If he had been born in a royal palace in a great city like Jerusalem, with all the symbols of wealth and prestige around him, we might, at best, admire him from a distance, queuing to catch a glimpse of him through the barred gates of the royal residence. At worst, we would dismiss him as unapproachable and irrelevant. But everything about the coming of Jesus proclaims his availability, especially to those who are poor in spirit. His very littleness and poverty somehow embrace us all.

He came to a small, out-of-the-way town. He was born in a comfortless animal shelter. His mother was a young woman who had no credentials other than obedience. His human father was a manual labourer. His first visitors were ordinary workers doing their dreary night duty out on the hills. His precarious safety in the early months depended on dreams and angelic visitations given to Joseph who was, thank God, a man of obedience (see *Matt 1:20; 2:13,19*). He lived as a refugee in Egypt for a time, then he grew up in Nazareth (*Matt 2:23*), another out-of-the-way town that was despised by many Jews for housing a Roman garrison. Later a disciple, Nathanael, spoke of Nazareth with a curl of his lips, 'Nazareth! Can anything good come from there?' (*John 1:46*).

Paul summed up the fragility and humbling of the Son of God in his hymn of praise written to believers at Philippi. He 'made himself nothing'... he was 'made in human likeness'... 'he humbled himself'... he 'became obedient to death' (*Phil 2:7,8*). It was in poverty and littleness that he came and to the empty-handed that he poured himself out.

Prayer

Lord, may your poured-out life continue to flow to the world through the open channel of my life today.

TUESDAY 11 DECEMBER

He Comes – In Flesh

John 1:14

'The Word became flesh and made his dwelling among us. We have seen his glory, the glory of the One and Only, who came from the Father, full of grace and truth' (v. 14, NIV).

'Deck the halls with boughs of holly' we sing. Why? Simply, 'Tis the season to be jolly!' So out come the tree, nativity scene, candles, a wreath on the front door, some frosted decorations stencilled onto the window, some lights up and over the roof. Dress it up, display it, deck it out, bigger and better and brighter than last year. Anything to cover the fact that when God got ready for Christmas, he undressed!

God stripped off his finery and appeared – how embarrassing – naked on the day he was born. He put aside status and honours, and appeared in the flesh of a newborn baby. When the gospel was first preached, the Romans said 'Impossible!' to the idea of a god becoming flesh. We say 'Impractical!' What do you do with a newborn baby, except hold it, change it, feed it, and let it captivate your heart? A newborn baby does not create revenue. It cannot be marketed or gift-wrapped. Santa Claus seems a much better commercial possibility with his jolly red suit and his bag full of goodies. And while S. C. disturbs the bank account and the pace of this month, that's all he disturbs. When all the gifts have been opened, he can be put back into storage and forgotten. God is not so easily dismissed.

God's heart of love moved him to make choices that seem strangely unstrategic. He came to shepherds, not to sovereigns. He came to a stable out the back, not to a five-star hotel. Wise men looked for him in Herod's palace but found him in a homely place. As the Word made flesh, coming to dwell among us, God has come closer than close, vulnerably one with us.

We need to resist the urge to cover God with Christmas. Let's prepare instead to celebrate the Feast of the Incarnation, with a God who tossed aside the tinsel and who identifies with our pain, our humanness, our flesh.

Veiled in flesh the Godhead see;
Hail the incarnate Deity!
Pleased as man with man to dwell,
Jesus, our Immanuel.

Charles Wesley, SASB 82

WEDNESDAY 12 DECEMBER

He Comes – Through a Real Family Line

Matthew 1:1–17

'A record of the genealogy of Jesus Christ the son of David, the son of Abraham' (v. 1, NIV).

I once watched a man act out these first verses of Matthew's Gospel. Some names he skimmed over, but with others a gesture, a look, an expression hinted at a story behind the name. For example, when he began with Abraham and Isaac (*v. 2*), he spoke with reverence. When he mentioned Rahab (*v. 5*), his face registered a strong hint of a shady story. When he came to 'Solomon, whose mother had been Uriah's wife' (*v. 6*), his voice expressed shock and scandal. When he came to the last verse in the list, '... Mary, of whom was born Jesus, who is called Christ' (*v. 16*), he folded his arms together as though he was holding a newborn baby and very gently laid it in the lap of a woman in the audience!

Such a dramatic presentation made a dry list come alive for me. But for those who first read this family line, the Jews to whom Matthew was writing, there would be nothing dry about it! This genealogy, throbbing with life and colour, is a roll-call of the Jewish nation. Luke's genealogy (see *Luke 3:23–28*) follows Mary, Jesus' blood relative, and traces her line right back to Adam, showing Jesus' relationship to the whole human race. Matthew's genealogy follows the line of Joseph, Jesus' legal father, and shows how Jesus was a descendant of Abraham, the father of all Jews.

Each name listed here has a story behind it. Some were heroes of the faith, like Abraham, Isaac, Ruth and David. Some had shady reputations, like Rahab and Tamar. Many were ordinary people, like Hezron, Ram and Nahshon. Others were downright evil, like Manasseh and Abijah.

This patchwork of names, representing glory and greatness, shadow and stain, is the record of our story as well. A study of our family line would no doubt reveal similar 'skeletons in the closet'. But the wonder is that God delights to work out his purposes in history through all kinds of people – ordinary, failing, sinful, striving, human people, just like you and me!

Celebrate this great news today!

THURSDAY 13 DECEMBER

He Comes – As a Gift

John 3:16–21

'Thanks be to God for his indescribable gift!' (2 Cor 9:15, NIV).

Ask a group of children in an affluent country what Christmas is all about and their enthusiastic response is likely to be 'Presents!' They're probably thinking of the bigger, brighter, better-than-ever toys and games that have been advertised for weeks on TV and in the junk mail, and upon which their hearts have been set.

This is a great commercial hijack, of course, for the heart of Christmas is indeed a gift, but not of the 'play now, pay later' variety. Christmas is Christmas simply and deeply because God gave. To unearth this truth may take some shovelling away of the trappings that so easily bury it during this month.

I recall with gratitude our first Christmas in Zambia. Away from the city, we saw no shops, no advertising, no Santa Claus. Decorations were home-made, gifts were simple – a ball of string, a roll of sellotape. Several of the 'aunties' on the mission station baked home-made cookies and wrapped them up for the children. Christmas carols were played from a boat on the middle of the Chikankata dam, the notes reaching the village huts nestled by the shoreline. Christmas dinner was a simple meal shared with friends. We read together the Christmas story from Luke's Gospel and let the sheer wonder of God's gift to the world touch us again. It was the most uncluttered and memorable Christmas I have ever known.

Christmas is not just presents and pudding, nuts and noise, turkey and tinsel. Christmas is also a time for silence and reflection, a time for memories and storytelling. Above all it is a time for wonder as we open our hearts again to God's gift.

When God gave, it was no 'virtual reality' gift, but real flesh and blood, for he came down the staircase of heaven with a baby in his arms and gave him to the world. No wonder Paul described this as a gift beyond description!

To reflect on

This year, is there a way you can simplify your giving and, in the process, celebrate God's gift to the world?

FRIDAY 14 DECEMBER

He Comes – Singing Glory

Luke 2:8–15

'Glory to God in the highest, and on earth peace to men on whom his favour rests' (v. 14, NIV).

'Do you know the song that the angels sang on that night in the long ago?' The songwriter A. P. Cobb poses the question and then proceeds to give the answer (*SASB* 80). The words of his chorus are taken directly from the song of the angels on the night when they appeared to the shepherds out in the fields. Their song had one resounding note – Glory!

The word 'glory' is rather hard to define. It seems to be used when other words are just not big enough but, like the word 'love', it has become blunted with overuse. So we speak of 'a glorious view from the aeroplane window' or 'a glorious rendition of an orchestral piece'. But the angels on that night had no difficulty with the word. It summed up everything they wanted to proclaim – praise, honour and worship. They acknowledged the grace and majesty of God in heaven for bringing peace to earth.

John, in his Gospel, looking through a different lens, used the same word to describe the coming of Jesus, the Word, the very expression of God. 'The Word became flesh and made his dwelling among us. We have seen his glory, the glory of the One and Only, who came from the Father, full of grace and truth' (*John 1:14*).

For Mary, that glory was translated into obedience which led to a birth in a lonely place, the care of a gift-child, the nurture of a young man and finally the surrender of her loved son to a most shameful death (see *John 19:25*). For Joseph, the glory of that birth announcement was lived out with work-worn hands that dutifully provided and cared for a son who was never really his, but just on loan.

We, too, who join in the song at this time of Advent, need to translate the glory into obedience, humility and loving service. And so we pray:

Lord Jesus, give me a humble, obedient heart that seeks only to glorify you. Help me to offer you my praise, my love and my service.

SATURDAY 15 DECEMBER

He Comes – To All Our Senses

Luke 2:1–20

'The shepherds returned, glorifying and praising God for all the things they had heard and seen, which were just as they had been told' (v. 20, NIV).

This month of December puts our senses on overload. The colours, tastes, fragrances, sounds and textures of Christmas can be a feast in more ways than one. But the gospel story can likewise be a feast for our senses – a truly sensuous experience – if we linger long enough. As we read Luke's account, it is like entering the wardrobe leading into Narnia. We are invited to step into the mystery.

Imagine you are reading this gospel story to a young child for the very first time. Read the words, but read also the colours and texture that lie behind the words. Or imagine you are the innkeeper's daughter, wakened by the brightness of a star shining right over your bedroom. You've crept out to the stable to see what's going on.

What do you hear?

- An angel song unlike anything you've ever heard before.
- The bleating of abandoned sheep.

What do you see?

- A heavenly display of glory that makes the millennium celebrations look like a fizzed firework.
- A young couple in drab surroundings, whose faces are flushed with joy and wonder.

What do you smell?

- The fragrance of the not-so-fragrant hay.
- The earthy smell of shepherd footwear, which would be forbidden in a modern hospital maternity ward.

What do you taste?

- A steaming hot drink brought in by the innkeeper's wife when she hears a baby crying.
- Salty tears as Mary weeps quietly with relief and weariness mingled with joy.

What do you feel?

- The rough wood of the manger that provides the first bed for this precious newborn.
- The so-soft skin of that baby's face.

Stay with the story as you go about the tasks of this day. Linger with your senses on full alert. In the midst of all the trimmings and trappings of Christmas, let the wonder of this story come alive for you again.

SUNDAY 16 DECEMBER

Third Sunday in Advent

Isaiah 61:1–11

'I delight greatly in the LORD; my soul rejoices in my God. For he has clothed me with garments of salvation and arrayed me in a robe of righteousness, as a bridegroom adorns his head like a priest, and as a bride adorns herself with her jewels' (v. 10, NIV).

Today is the third Sunday in Advent and the third purple candle, representing joy, is lit. The candles of hope and peace are also lit again, as a reminder of God's gifts.

The book of Isaiah describes the joy that will come with the dawning of God's realm of peace and righteousness. The signs will be obvious – the broken-hearted will be healed, captives will be set free, justice will be available to all and sadness will turn to joy. God's people will toss aside the heavy garments of mourning and be clothed with new garments of salvation. It will be an exchange of beauty for ashes. In reading these verses, I'm reminded of my daughter who, when she was very little, sat one evening, fresh from the bath and with her fair curls soft and fragrant, and sang with joy, 'He gave me beautiful rashes'!

Jesus applied the words of promise from Isaiah 61:1–2 to himself when he spoke in the synagogue at Nazareth (see *Luke 4:16–21*). What Isaiah foretold, Jesus fulfilled. He came with good news for the poor, sight for the blind, freedom for those captured by sin, joy to replace sorrow. His coming was indeed 'Joy to the world!'

The apostle Paul emphasised the message of joy. This man who knew persecution, imprisonment, shipwreck, church fights and death threats from the inside, urged those who follow Jesus to 'Be joyful always' (*1 Thess 5:16*). He knew that joy had little to do with circumstances and everything to do with attitude. It could be found in the roughest seas or the dankest prison.

In a world where bad news hits the headlines every day, we need to hear a message of joy, now more than ever. Look for opportunities this Advent to comfort someone who is broken-hearted, to restore a relationship, to fill with good things someone who is hungry, and to let God's joy flow through you out into the world.

Prayer

Loving God, light a candle of joy in my life this Advent and let its warmth spread to those around me.

MONDAY 17 DECEMBER

He Comes – Ready or Not

Matthew 2:1–8, 16

'When he had called together all the people's chief priests and teachers of the law, he asked them where the Christ was to be born' (v. 4, NIV).

Do you remember playing 'Hide and Seek' when you were young? One person hides while the other keeps their eyes (more or less!) shut and counts up to an agreed number. Then the cry, 'I'm coming, ready or not!'

I'm reminded of that game when I read the account of Herod's dealings with the Magi who came to Jerusalem, looking for the newborn king of the Jews. When Herod heard this, he was disturbed. After all, anyone with a royal title was immediately a threat to his throne. He called his chief priests and teachers of the law to find out the location of the birthplace. Being well versed in Scriptures, they knew exactly where to look – in Micah's prophecy. Next, he called the Magi to find out the exact time of the star's appearance. He then sent them on to Bethlehem, asking that they return to report to him, 'so that I too may go and worship him'.

These few verses give three different reactions to Jesus' coming. Herod mouthed words of worship, but his heart was fixed on murder, as is clearly seen when the months passed and the Magi did not return. Realising that he had been outwitted, he gave his grisly order for all the male children in Bethlehem, two years old and under, to be put to death.

The chief priests and teachers of the law knew the words of Scripture, but their hearts were indifferent to knowing the One of whom the Scripture spoke. If they had really cared, they would have been off to nearby Bethlehem like a shot, looking for the one promised hundreds of years earlier and now reported to have been born. In contrast, the Magi came from great distance, and presumably at great cost, for the sole purpose of worshipping the child King.

There are still today those who love Jesus, those who hate him and those who couldn't care less. But to all he comes, whether we are 'ready or not', offering a way of forgiveness and love.

To reflect on

Hostility, indifference or worship – which characterises you?

TUESDAY 18 DECEMBER

He Comes – To Zechariah

Luke 1:5–25

'But the angel said to him: "Do not be afraid, Zechariah; your prayer has been heard. Your wife Elizabeth will bear you a son, and you are to give him the name John" ' (v. 13, NIV).

This was a day of days for Zechariah. Although he had been a priest for years, being a direct descendant of Aaron, he may have never before had the opportunity to go into the temple to burn incense on behalf of the people. With so many descendants of Aaron, each division of priests would be on duty for just one week twice a year, and the duties would be allocated by lot.

What might Zechariah be thinking as he carried out his task? 'Wait till I tell Elizabeth about this!' 'If only I had a son to share the joy of this day!' Whatever his thoughts, they were interrupted by the appearance of an angel who spoke a promise that a son, 'a joy and delight' (*v. 14*), would be born to him and Elizabeth. This son would be no ordinary person. He would be great in the sight of God, subject to the Nazirite vow of abstinence (*Num 6:1–4*), and filled with the Holy Spirit from the time of his birth. He would have the spirit and power of Elijah and the task of preparing the way for the Messiah.

Stunned, Zechariah stammered his response. 'But how . . . ?' How could such a momentous thing happen to him and his elderly wife? Silenced for his unbelief and in a daze of joy and wonder, Zechariah eventually came out of the temple, but was unable to pronounce the Aaronic blessing over the waiting worshippers. At the end of his time of service, he returned home.

During his months of silence, as the baby John grew inside Elizabeth's womb, did faith grow inside Zechariah? Did he discover, even in his old age, that he too could at last believe all the words that he had said over the years as he carried the people's needs and prayers to God? Did he see at his infant son's birth that God's redemption was real, and that it had come right into his own home?

Prayer

Lord God, give me eyes to see the signs of your redemption all around me.

WEDNESDAY 19 DECEMBER

He Comes – To Elizabeth

Luke 1:23–25, 39–45, 57–58

' "The Lord has done this for me," she said. "In these days he has shown his favour and taken away my disgrace among the people" ' (v. 25, NIV).

How did the mute Zechariah tell Elizabeth about his angelic visitation in the temple when he got home? Sign language would seem rather inadequate to convey such a momentous message. Did he write her a note? 'Dear Elizabeth, I know you're going to find this rather hard to believe, but . . .' And what was her reaction when she did finally understand? Did she laugh as loudly as Sarah laughed when she was told of her child who would be born, long past her childbearing years?

How did aged Elizabeth, familiar with arthritic knees and failing eyesight, now cope with an unfamiliar morning sickness? How did fingers that had lost their suppleness manage to make baby garments? How did this woman who had carried the stigma of childlessness all her married life cope with the movements of the child she now carried in her womb?

For the first five months of her pregnancy she remained in seclusion. Was that out of embarrassment ('Whatever will the girls at the Gardening Group say?'), or out of sheer joy and gratitude that rendered her as speechless as Zechariah? But news travelled fast among the family. Seventy miles away in Nazareth, Elizabeth's cousin Mary also unexpectedly became pregnant. Within days of her angelic visitation, Mary went to visit Elizabeth. These two women, one aged and having abandoned any dream of childrearing, and the other not yet married and thus not quite ready for the task, were bound together by the unique gifts that God had given them. One would be the mother of the Saviour of the world; the other, of his messenger.

As they shared their wonder and dreamed their dreams together, could they have any idea of what lay ahead for them and for their sons? Could they possibly know that their days of joy and glory would be woven together with great and terrible days? And would they have changed anything if they had known?

Prayer

When dreams lie faded and hopes are gone, when sadness puts wrinkles on my heart, Lord, help me to remember Elizabeth.

THURSDAY 20 DECEMBER

He Comes – To Joseph

Matthew 1:18–25

'Because Joseph her husband was a righteous man and did not want to expose her to public disgrace, he had in mind to divorce her quietly' (v. 19, NIV).

He's the forgotten character of the Christmas story. While the spotlight naturally falls on Mary and her dramatic part in it all, Joseph stands slightly back in the shadows. But he was a real man, confronted with a very real dilemma. Mary and Joseph were betrothed to be married. This arrangement was a formal and binding contract, entered into before witnesses, and broken only by divorce. During this time they would be known as husband and wife even though the public marriage ceremony had not yet taken place and Mary would still be living with her own family.

With the news of Mary's pregnancy came Joseph's dilemma. Being 'a righteous man', he did not want to expose Mary as an adulteress, yet neither would he marry one so obviously guilty of sin. He therefore chose the only other option open to him: formal divorce proceedings in relative privacy, where only two witnesses would be required.

While Joseph pondered his situation, no doubt going over and over the details, an angel of the Lord appeared to him in a dream, with a revelation that threw an entirely new light on Mary's pregnancy. The protestations of innocence that she had doubtless made to Joseph were now seen to be true.

'Do not be afraid to take Mary home as your wife,' he was told, 'because what is conceived in her is from the Holy Spirit' (*v. 20*). Both Mary and Joseph had passive roles in this life-changing event. God had initiated it all. 'She will . . . you are to . . . because he will . . .' (*v. 21*). Yet Joseph had a part to play which was just as important as Mary's was. Joseph did what he was commanded, formalising the marriage, taking Mary to his own home but honouring her virginity. At the birth of her baby, Joseph named him Jesus, indicating the formal adoption of the child into the line of David.

To reflect on

Joseph stands in the story as a man of honour, respectful of Mary, obedient to the divine command. Could it be said that he too 'bore' the child?

FRIDAY 21 DECEMBER

He Comes – To an Innkeeper

Luke 2:1–7

'. . . there was no room for them in the inn' (v. 7, NIV).

He's easy to miss, this person in the Advent narrative. He's not even mentioned in Scripture, just there by suggestion. But in children's nativity pageants down through the ages, the innkeeper has been portrayed as a villain second only to Herod, beer-bellied (that was his business after all!), rough, gruff and far from welcoming.

He obviously wasn't waiting for a young couple with heaven in their hearts. He wasn't into entertaining 'angels without knowing it' (*Heb 13:2*). All he knew was that the inn was chock-a-block full. It was census time after all, and Bethlehem was as packed as if it had been hosting the World Cup! But afterwards, once the dust of the shepherds' sandals had settled and news got round, did this man not have some pensive moments?

'Well, it wasn't my fault, everyone seems to blame me. What else could I do? It was either the stable or back out onto the street. I can't make walls stretch when they're already bulging. I can't do the impossible. In fact I thought I was being generous, letting them use the stable. After all, it's warm and sheltered out there, even if it is a bit smelly. People just have to put up with that if they turn up at the last minute. I gave them the best I had, can't do more than that, surely!

'But that woman, the look she had on her face, it still bothers me. I can't sleep, thinking about her. Oh, she was grateful enough to have somewhere to rest, I know, but there was something more. It was like a look of pity or sorrow for me. But why? She was the one to be pitied, so young and about to be a mother, poor girl.

'Then when they left a few days ago, her words to me were strange. I still can't work it out. She said, "Give the child more than the stable of your heart!" Strange that!'

Prayer

Lord, help me to give you more than the stable of my heart.

SATURDAY 22 DECEMBER

He Comes – To Mary

Luke 1:26–38, 46–55

' "I am the Lord's servant," Mary answered. "May it be to me as you have said" ' (v. 38, NIV).

The angel addressed her as 'highly favoured'. Elizabeth called her 'blessed'. Mary probably felt neither when the angel first appeared. After all, she was young, poor and female – all the characteristics that would be thought to disqualify her for any special favour from God. But in spite of who she was – or because of who she was – God chose her to be the human mother of his Son. Mary's response, 'How will this be since I am a virgin?' (*v. 34*), was not one of disbelief. It was a purely practical, if somewhat embarrassing question. The angel answered, telling her about Elizabeth who was also pregnant. It seems that Mary wasted no time in going to visit her relative. After all, if it was true about the older woman, then it was gloriously, awesomely true about herself as well! Imagine these two women, the lives of both turned upside down by divine intervention, running into each other's arms in an embrace of human comfort.

Mary's Magnificat, her psalm of praise, echoes Hannah's song when she brings her long-awaited son to the temple (*1 Sam 2:1–10*). As Mary waits for her promised son, she joins with the whole nation of Israel waiting for its promised Messiah.

But it will not all be glory. Caesar Augustus orders a census by tribe and family. Those of David's line must register in David's city, Bethlehem. There are no exceptions, even for a young woman in the last stages of pregnancy. It is inconvenient, impractical and dangerous, but in an occupied land there is nothing to do but obey. Not the freely given obedience of love and trust (*v. 38*), but the obedience of fear and force.

Mary would be exhausted by the journey, wearied further at having to try inn after inn, and at last grateful for a bed in a cave. There is no midwife in attendance, no comforting words of experience to help her. Just Joseph. In this poor place, God comes.

To reflect on

There is no door on this cave. It is open to anyone.

SUNDAY 23 DECEMBER

Fourth Sunday in Advent

John 3:16–21

'For God so loved the world that he gave his one and only Son, that whoever believes in him shall not perish but have eternal life' (v. 16, NIV).

Today is the fourth Sunday in Advent and the rose-coloured candle representing love is lit. The previous candles of hope, peace and joy are lit once more as well.

With every gift that we prepare this Christmas, the wrapping will soon be tossed aside so that the gift inside can be revealed. There may be a toddler who is more interested in the crunching sound of the paper than the gift it contains, or a frugal mum who will carefully fold the paper for another time. But, for most of us, the wrapping is of little interest, to be torn open and discarded as quickly as possible.

The wrapping of God's gift to us, however, is the most important part. Jesus came wrapped up in flesh or, as a recent songwriter put it, 'He came special delivery, wrapped up in love.' The wrapping of this God-gift takes us to the very heart of the mystery.

The Jewish people, looking for the Messiah, thought he would come on a charging warhorse with all the signs of warfare and victory in attendance. There would be colour, noise and spectacle about his coming. That's why so many missed him. He came in the golden glow of a star hung silently over a dark cave. He came in the cry of a young woman giving birth to her first baby. The only real spectacle that attended his birth took place out on a nearby hillside where an angelic choir entertained some common shepherds. These were the sounds of love breaking into the world. In this child, God wrapped himself in flesh, took on our struggles and temptations and identified with our humanity. This was the way he chose to be one with us, Immanuel.

God's gift of love is offered to us again this Christmas. For all who receive him, the call is to keep on unwrapping this gift and passing it on and out to a world that needs love, now more than ever.

Prayer

O come let us adore him, Christ the Lord!

MONDAY 24 DECEMBER

He Comes – In the Fullness of Time

Luke 2:1–7

'When the time had fully come, God sent his Son, born of a woman . . .' (Gal 4:4, NIV).

There is a time for everything, the teacher of Ecclesiastes tells us, 'a time to be born and a time to die'. That's not too difficult for us to understand, creatures of time that we are. From birth to death, our lives are shaped by the age into which we are born and the events that happen as we grow. Clocks and calendars become the marker points of our life-story. 'At 2.30 this afternoon I did . . .' or 'When I was ten, I went . . .' This is 'chronos' time, the steady, invariable passing of one moment after another.

When it comes to God, we know that he is not bound by time in the way that we are. He is eternal, the one who always was, who is and who always will be. But Advent reminds us of the marvel that the one who created time chose to come and live within time. At a moment in history that can be pinpointed, Jesus was born. Luke gives the broad strokes of when it happened – Caesar Augustus was the Roman emperor and Quirinius was the governor of Syria (*vv. 1–2*).

He came and he had a birthday, like every other newborn baby, but this was more than God's chronos time. This was also God's 'kairos' time, a moment of deep significance and promise. Chronos time is the beating of a metronome or the ticking of a clock. Kairos time is the beating of God's heart.

In the birth of Jesus, kairos met chronos, eternity touched earth, God came and took hold of us with the hand of a baby. The moment of his birth sliced history in two – before and after – but the significance of his incarnation cannot be measured in tidy hours and minutes. The story of his birth in a comfortless cave in Bethlehem is the story that gives meaning to our lives. This story is gospel – good news – whose ending is not death but resurrection.

To reflect on

O wonder of wonders that none can unfold
The Ancient of Days is an hour or two old.

H. R. Bramley

TUESDAY 25 DECEMBER

He Comes – Singing Love

Luke 2:1–7

'This is how much God loved the world: He gave his Son, his one and only Son. And this is why: so that no one need be destroyed; by believing in him, anyone can have a whole and lasting life' (John 3:16, *The Message*).

The dark night wakes, the glory breaks
and Christmas comes once more!

Today the white Christ-candle, standing at the centre of the Advent wreath, is lit. The surrounding candles of hope, peace, joy and love are relit. Today all the promises of God find their fulfilment in Jesus.

Three small wood-carved figures stand in the nativity scene. On Mary's face, a look of contentment. The rigours of the long journey and the loneliness of giving birth are forgotten. As she gazes at her son she says again, 'May it be to me as you have said' (*Luke 1:38*). On Joseph's face, a mixture of wonder and worry. 'Who is this child?' 'Why have I been chosen to care for him?' On the baby's face, a resting, a peace.

A beam of light shines onto the three figures, illuminating their faces and throwing their shadows onto the wall. They are no longer small. Now they are large, hopeful figures, outlined with majesty and glory, standing strongly on the walls of our life and our world. The shadows from those three figures continue to be thrown onto the walls of ghettos and gang houses, brothels and bars, shanty towns and factories all round the world. Wherever those shadows fall, people's lives are changed, sometimes quietly, sometimes dramatically, for wherever people are, God is. This is the heart of Christmas, the most wonderful gift of all. This is what people everywhere and in various ways celebrate on this day.

He comes again today, offering the way of peace to war-torn hearts, families and nations. He comes, bringing light to those living in darkness. He comes, bringing hope to those who have lost all hope. He comes with joy to those who have grown used to the colours of sorrow. He comes, singing his song of love.

O holy Child of Bethlehem,
Descend to us, we pray;
Cast out our sin, and enter in,
Be born in us today.

Phillips Brooks, SASB 86

WEDNESDAY 26 DECEMBER

He Comes – To Shepherds

Luke 2:8–20

'When the angels had left them and gone into heaven, the shepherds said to one another, "Let's go to Bethlehem and see this thing that has happened, which the Lord has told us about" ' (v. 15, NIV).

The first people to hear the announcement of the birth of Mary's baby were not her parents back in Nazareth, but a group of unknown shepherds, out on the hills near Bethlehem. The constant demands of their task of guarding the flocks against thieves and predators meant that shepherds were unable to observe many of the regulations of the law, such as hand-washing. So the religious despised them as common. But it was to these rough and common men, and not to the religious, that the angels came. These shepherds, used to the ways of lambs destined for sacrifice in the temple, were invited to greet the Lamb of God who would be sacrificed for the sins of the world.

They were scared out of their wits at the angelic host that came to tell them the news. They had not been expecting angels! They sat in dazed awe as the heavenly choir sang its Gloria. Then they hurried to find the place where the child was. They came empty-handed to the cave. There they stood in wonder before a newborn baby, unwashed and wrinkled, in an animal's feedbox. They saw his mother sleeping in exhaustion. They saw a man with shining eyes, guarding the treasure entrusted to him. They came in and saw, then with wonder and joy, they went out to tell.

Would a night out on the hills ever be the same again? How often would that story be repeated? 'Remember the night the angels came? Remember the baby, how he looked? Remember the reaction when we told our wives and the others in the village? They thought we'd been drinking! Remember . . . ?'

In today's language, it would be to young boys tending a group of work-worn cattle out on a Zambian hillside, or to scrub-cutters in the outbacks of Australia, that he comes. For the simple, the uncluttered, even the unexpecting, God at times reserves his greatest surprises, his most wondrous gifts.

What can I give Him, poor as I am?
If I were a shepherd, I would bring a lamb . . .

Christina Rossetti

THURSDAY 27 DECEMBER

He Comes – To Wise Men

Matthew 2:1–12

'On coming to the house, they saw the child with his mother Mary, and they bowed down and worshipped him. Then they opened their treasures and presented him with gifts of gold and of incense and of myrrh' (v. 11, NIV).

They're familiar figures, these three, an essential part of every nativity pageant. They come with stars in their eyes, wearing silken gowns from the drama cupboard and kingly crowns slightly dented from their long journey by camel-back. Their rich gifts sparkle with sequins and gold braid.

The reality of these foreign visitors was probably quite different from what we have become used to, but some things seem certain. They came from a long way away, arriving some months after the baby's birth. They naturally looked first for the king of the Jews in the Jewish capital, Jerusalem. They were educated, complicated and foreign. These were men who gained insight into world affairs by their observation of the planets and stars. They were Gentiles, but as welcome at this birth as the chosen people of God.

In contrast to the shepherds, they came both full-hearted and full-handed. We think of them as three, because three gifts were mentioned: gold, incense and myrrh. Seekers who would come bringing such gifts were obviously men of wealth. But for all their wealth and learning, the homage with which they knelt before Jesus indicated that they knew they were in the presence of someone far greater than themselves. The gold was a gift to royalty, for he was a King. The incense was a gift to deity, for he was God. Myrrh was a gift to humanity, for he was a man. It was a burial spice, so even at his birth, the fragrance of suffering could be detected.

This passage is full of colour and contrast. Herod, his status as king threatened by the news of the birth of one who is to be king of the Jews, lashes out with unrestrained frenzy and terrifying slaughter (*vv. 16–18*). Jesus, newborn King of the Jews, lies contentedly in his mother's arms, awaiting his next feed.

What can I give him, poor as I am?...
If I were a wise man, I would do my part;
Yet what can I give him? Give him my heart!

Christina Rossetti

FRIDAY 28 DECEMBER

He Comes – With Tears

Matthew 2:13–18

'A voice is heard in Ramah, weeping and great mourning,
Rachel weeping for her children and refusing to be comforted,
because they are no more' (v. 18, NIV).

This day is traditionally celebrated as the 'Day of the Holy Innocents' in remembrance of Herod's frenzied slaughter of all the boys in Bethlehem and its vicinity who were two years old and under. This account is one of stark contrasts. There are stars and swords, kingly visitations and kingly agitation, Mary rejoicing and Rachel weeping, the children who die and the Child who gets away.

Herod the Great had been appointed ruler of the Jews in 40BC. He was a cruel monarch, an Idumaean, not a Jew. He committed many atrocities during his reign, including the slaughter of some of his own children in order to make his throne secure. Outraged that the visiting Magi had not returned to tell him where the 'king of the Jews' could be found, and terrified that this king would one day take his place, Herod gave his grisly order.

The number of children killed was probably about twenty. Matthew quotes the prophet Jeremiah, and Rachel who expresses the anguish of all the mothers of Bethlehem. Ramah was where the Jews gathered before they were carried off into exile in Babylon. Jesus, meantime, is carried off by his protective parents, in response to a dream, to the safety of Egypt.

The aching question must be answered – why did God save him, but not the other boys? Why were their protective parents not granted a warning dream? Why does a three-year-old playing at the park suddenly die of a genetic disorder? Why does a newspaper headline scream the story of yet another toddler beaten to death? Why did Dunblane happen?

There are suffering innocents not far from us at any time. Rachel and the mothers of Bethlehem continue to weep their tears. The comfort in this stark account is that Jesus, the child who 'got away', came back to atone for the blood of those children and their mothers' tears. 'God with us' embraces the innocents of every age.

Pray today for young victims of famine, homelessness, warfare and neglect.

SATURDAY 29 DECEMBER

He Comes – To John

Luke 3:1–6

'The word of God came to John son of Zechariah in the desert' (v. 2, NIV).

God's word came not to Emperor Tiberias, not to Pontius Pilate nor Herod, not even to Annas and Caiaphas, the high priests. These were the most powerful leaders in Palestine. But God's word did not come to them. He bypassed the important people, the governors and celebrities, even the institutional church, to speak to a strange prophet from rural Judea, known for his strange diet and even stranger dress sense (see *Mark 1:6*). The word of God came to John, son of Zechariah, in the desert, a nobody in the middle of nowhere. Through this man, the prophet Isaiah's words would be fulfilled. Through this way-preparer, path-straightener, the Lord would come. Through this man, amazing as it might seem, 'all mankind will see God's salvation'.

Still today, God's word often comes through the 'desert' people, the strange ones in our midst. They are the ones without status or voice. We think of them as 'God's little people'. They are poor people. Bag ladies. Sick people. People of other races. People with physical or mental disabilities. Young children. Old people. Through these people, God's salvation is often seen and heard a little more clearly than through those who have their words as polished as their Sunday shoes.

In a corps where my husband and I were in charge, one of the regular attenders on a Sunday morning was a young man with Down's syndrome. When the opportunity was given for someone to lead the meeting in prayer, this young man was often first on his feet. His words were difficult to understand, but the reverence with which he took off his cap and held it as he prayed, and the spirit of his prayer, on many occasions brought us into the very presence of God.

Part of our Advent watch this year has been to look for God's coming to us in the unexpected places, and to recognise God's word in unexpected people. May our eyes stay open to recognise and welcome him!

Prayer

God of surprises, keep on surprising us with all the unexpected ways in which you come!

SUNDAY 30 DECEMBER

He Comes – With Salvation

Luke 2:22–38

'Sovereign Lord, as you have promised, you now dismiss your servant in peace. For my eyes have seen your salvation' (vv. 29,30, NIV).

They were a long-sighted pair, Simeon and Anna. Years of waiting and watching for what they knew had been promised but had not yet seen, had quietened their hearts and put the eyes of their faith on full alert. When Simeon saw Mary and Joseph bringing the child Jesus into the temple for dedication (see *Exod 13:12*), he knew that this was the one he had been waiting for. His song of praise is called *Nunc Dimittis,* the Latin translation of his words 'Now dismiss . . .' Having seen the Messiah, the fulfilment of his years of waiting, Simeon could now die in peace.

He rejoiced that this child was the salvation of God in the flesh. He would bring glory to God's chosen people, for all eyes would be drawn to Israel through what the Messiah would do. He would also be a light bringing revelation to the Gentiles, for they would be brought into blessing through his ministry.

But not all the notes of Simeon's song of praise are joyful. He predicted that Jesus would split the nation in two. Some would rise because of him but some would fall. Some would receive him while others would reject him. Turning to Mary, Simeon warned her that the opposition her son faced would bring her great pain. The aged Anna then spoke. Having lived her life in continuous intercession, she too recognised God's salvation and redemption in this child.

Simeon and Anna stand at the end of a long line of people who welcomed the Christ child. Angels, the young mother, Joseph, common shepherds, righteous elderly and foreign Magi – all had a part to play, and a voice of welcome and recognition. This child Jesus has come bringing salvation to people of all ages, all races and all classes. Peter tells us that for those who reject him, he is a stumbling block, but for those who receive him, he is a cornerstone upon whom a solid life can be built (*1 Pet 2:6–8*).

Praise God, he comes with salvation for you and me today!

MONDAY 31 DECEMBER

He Comes – And Is Still Coming!

1 Corinthians 15:51–58

' "I am the Alpha and the Omega," says the Lord God, "who is, and who was, and who is to come, the Almighty" ' (Rev 1:8, NIV).

The last day of the year is a good time to take stock. It is like climbing to the top of a hill, looking back over the track that has brought us to this point, then looking forward to where the path takes us next. As we come to the close of the Advent series, I wonder what glimpses of God's coming you have caught along the way. Have there been graced moments when he has come, unexpectedly transforming an ordinary incident into something special? Have there been unlikely people who have brought a reminder of God's love to you? What have you seen during these weeks of waiting and watching?

While we wrap up a year, and a series, it may be helpful to remember that calendars or clocks do not confine God. He has come, but still he is coming. In considering his first coming, we see signs of his second coming. The good news of Advent reminds us of what took place and prepares us for what is yet to take place. We look back in reflection, and forward in expectation.

The first time he came, it was via a woman's womb, with a very restricted audience.
The next time he comes, every eye will see him.
The first time he came as a baby, the Lamb of God.
The next time he is coming as the Lion of the tribe of Judah.
The first time he came in poverty, to a stark cave.
The next time he is coming in power.
The first time he came to die.
The next time he will raise the dead.
The first time he came in meekness.
The next time he is coming in majesty.
The first time he came as the king of the Jews.
The next time he is coming as the King of kings!

The Christ has come! Welcome him!
The King is coming! Worship him!

NOTES

1 Graham Kendrick, 'All I once held dear', copyright ©1993 Make Way Music, PO Box 263, Croydon, Surrey, CR9 5AP, UK. International copyright secured. All rights reserved. Used by permission.
2 Roy Hicks, 'Praise the name of Jesus!', copyright ©1976 Latter Rain Music, 8025 Deering Avenue, Canoga Park, California 91304, USA.
3 Tanya Riches, 'Jesus, what a beautiful name!', copyright ©1995 Tanya Riches/Hillsongs Publishing. Administered by Kingsway's Thankyou Music, P.O. Box 75, Eastbourne, East Sussex BN23 6NW, UK, for UK and Europe. Used by permission.
4 Sophie Conty/Naomi Batya, 'King of Kings and Lord of Lords', copyright ©1980 Maranatha! Music, PO Box 1396, Costa Mesa, CA 92626, USA.
5 Mavis Ford, 'Hosanna to the Son of David', copyright ©1978 Word's Spirit of Praise Music. Administered by CopyCare, P.O. Box 77, Hailsham, BN27 3EF, music@copycare.com and used by permission.
6 Edith Schaeffer, *Affliction*, Hodder & Stoughton, 1978.
7 Charles Swindoll, *Growing Strong in the Seasons of Life*, ANZEA Publishers, 1983.

INDEX
(as from: Pentecost 1996)

Words of Life Bible reading notes
are published three times a year:

Easter
(January–April)

Pentecost
(May–August)

Advent
(September–December)

In each edition you will find:

- informative commentary
- a wide variety of Bible passages
- topics for praise and prayer
- points to ponder
- cross references for further study

Why not place a regular order for *Words of Life*?
Collect each volume and build a lasting resource
for personal or group study.